Isaiah's Leper

Isaiah's Leper

A Catholic Asks the Question: "Would Jesus Have Anything to do With the Roman Catholic Church?"

George D. O'Clock, Ph.D.

iUniverse, Inc.
New York Lincoln Shanghai

Isaiah's Leper
A Catholic Asks the Question: "Would Jesus Have Anything to do With the Roman Catholic Church?"

Copyright © 2005 by George D. O'Clock, Jr.

All rights reserved. No part of this book may be used or reproduced by any means, graphic, electronic, or mechanical, including photocopying, recording, taping or by any information storage retrieval system without the written permission of the publisher except in the case of brief quotations embodied in critical articles and reviews.

iUniverse books may be ordered through booksellers or by contacting:

iUniverse
2021 Pine Lake Road, Suite 100
Lincoln, NE 68512
www.iuniverse.com
1-800-Authors (1-800-288-4677)

Registered Copyright, Registration Number Txu1-174-173
Copyright Office, Washington, D.C.

ISBN-13: 978-0-595-35141-1 (pbk)
ISBN-13: 978-0-595-67205-9 (cloth)
ISBN-13: 978-0-595-79843-8 (ebk)
ISBN-10: 0-595-35141-7 (pbk)
ISBN-10: 0-595-67205-1 (cloth)
ISBN-10: 0-595-79843-8 (ebk)

Printed in the United States of America

"Who hath believed our report?

And to whom is the arm of the Lord revealed? And he shall grow up as a tender plant before him and as a root out of a thirsty ground: there is no beauty in him, nor comeliness: and we have seen him, and there was no sightliness, that we should be desirous of him. Despised, and the most abject of men, a man of sorrows and acquainted with infirmity: and his look was as it were hidden and despised, whereupon we esteemed him not. Surely he hath borne our infirmities and carried our sorrows: and WE HAVE THOUGHT HIM AS IT WERE A LEPER, and as one struck by God and afflicted. But he was wounded for our iniquities, he was bruised for our sins: the chastisement of our peace was upon him, AND BY HIS BRUISES WE ARE HEALED."

Isaiah 53: 1-5

I dedicate this book to the victims. And, there are millions of them.

"Knowledge speaks, but wisdom listens." Jimi Hendrix (1942–1970)

CONTENTS

ACKNOWLEDGEMENTS xi
PREFACE xiii
1. INTRODUCTION 1
2. DISCOVERING THE "VILLAIN" THAT JESUS DESCRIBES 5
3. QUESTIONS AND CONCERNS THAT WILL NEVER GO AWAY 8
4. WHAT ARE THE CONCERNS EXPRESSED BY PRIESTS,
   NUNS AND LAITY? 12
5. WHAT IS THE FUNDAMENTAL FLAW IN MOST
   ORGANIZED RELIGIONS? 25
6. DOES THE ROMAN CATHOLIC CHURCH FOLLOW
   THE BASIC TEACHINGS OF JESUS? 35
7. IS THE ROMAN CATHOLIC CHURCH THE ONE TRUE
   CHURCH ESTABLISHED BY JESUS? 46
8. IS THE PAPAL LINE UNBROKEN AND INFALLIBLE
   (EX CATHEDRA)? 52
9. CATHOLIC CANON LAW: DOES IT HAVE A VALID
   FOUNDATION? 62
10. CAN THE ROMAN CATHOLIC CHURCH SAVE ITS OWN SOUL? 67
11. HOW MIGHTY IS GOD ALMIGHTY? 74
12. AS I GET CLOSER TO JESUS, WHY DO I DRIFT FURTHER
    AWAY FROM THE ROMAN CATHOLIC CHURCH? 84
13. WHERE CAN A DISSENTING CATHOLIC GO FROM HERE? 88

"If you don't know where you are going, you will wind up somewhere else."
Yogi Berra

14. THE NINTH LEPER 98
REFERENCES 111
ABOUT THE AUTHOR 117

"The world is my country, all mankind are my brethren, and to do good is my religion." Thomas Paine (1737–1809)

ACKNOWLEDGEMENTS

I owe a debt of gratitude to so many. In discussions concerning this effort, I am often surprised to see "who comes out of the woodwork." They are friends, casual acquaintances, students, teachers, priests, nuns, family members and many people who are simply interested. For obvious reasons, their names will not appear in this book. In some cases, certain names do appear. But, I am simply citing their work, or mentioning something that they did, to show how they have inspired me. None of them should be labeled as a "participant."

A number of references are cited. Two of the primary sources of information for this book are the Bible (Douay Rheims version, for the most part) and the Catholic Encyclopedia. The areas that I target in the Catholic Encyclopedia are those containing elaborate excuses and justifications for hierarchical and papal actions considered to be corrupt, brutal or criminal. A wealth of information concerning these "actions" is available in Catholic university and Catholic high school libraries. These additional sources can provide the objectivity and balance needed to see through the excuses and self deception that often seem to be characteristics of official and approved Catholic information.

This book makes frequent use of the National Catholic Reporter as a reference for articles concerning corrupt practices in the Roman Catholic Church. As a credible source, there is none better than the National Catholic Reporter (NCR). NCR addressed the pedophile priest scandal long before it became a news focus. In the early 1980's, while other Catholic sources and the U.S. news media were suppressing stories on this kind of depravity, NCR had the courage to reveal the horrible truth. There are very few publications (Catholic or secular) that can even come close to matching NCR's timing, journalistic integrity and truthfulness with respect to exposing sexual, financial and political scandals in the Roman Catholic Church.

"A clear conscience is usually the sign of a bad memory." Stephen Wright

PREFACE

If this book has any merit, it should serve as a catalyst to promote further investigation on the part of the reader. Think of this book as an eye-opener, study guide, reference point or something to dispute. I have attempted to give a message of hope and encouragement to Catholics who are struggling with an organization that has betrayed them. There is some attention paid, and direction given, with respect to an alternative. However, this book has not been designed to present a "substantial alternative" to Roman Catholicism. That would be "putting the cart before the horse." At this point, we have to carefully examine and analyze policies and actions of the Roman Catholic Church that violate the teachings and values of Jesus. If we do not pay enough attention to these details, a substantial alternative could be just as corrupt and invalid as the present one.

Hopefully, this book can provide an antidote to help counteract justifications and excuses that are given for the corruption, persecution and victimization that often accompany religious dogma and religious practices. The Inquisition has been an excellent excuse generator. In his book, *The Church and I* (Doubleday (1974)), Frank Sheed appears to brush aside Roman Church sanctioned slaughter, theft and depravity by suggesting that the Inquisition was not a bloodbath, but more of "a defect of vision," "driven by the love of God" and could be considered "normal punishment for public crimes." Sheed suggests that the Church should be "judged, not by the sinners, not even by the average; but by the saints" and the Church should be "judged only by those who know its teachings, obey its laws and receive its sacraments." This is the kind of logic and reasoning that can be used to nourish a self-serving and corrupt organization. The issue often not addressed is that some of these "saints" appear to have been, in one way or another, quite corrupt; with their alleged involvement in murder, adultery, bribery, financial misdeeds, etc.

> "Men never do evil so completely and cheerfully as when they do it from religious conviction." Blaise Pascal (1623–1662)

For example, Cardinal John Henry Newman (1801–1890) had to give up trying to justify St. Cyril's actions because of Cyril's penchant for violence and bloodshed and Cyril's participation in hastening the death of St. John Chrysostom. Also, St. Cyril was not too shy about engaging in various forms of bribery (Cyril's "golden arrows") in order to get his way. St. Damasus was brought to trial for adultery (apparently, he had quite a reputation). St. Jerome appears to have implicated Damasus I as a contributing factor for the corruption in the Church of Rome. St. Callistus served time in the Sardinian mines for misappropriation of funds in a banking scandal. St. Leo I was alleged to have engaged in torture. If the Church is to be judged only by saints and hard-core followers of the Roman Catholic Church, this would imply that only the foxes should be allowed to guard the hen house. This kind of oversight produces very limited accountability and has contributed to various Vatican bank scandals, alleged Church participation in war crimes, persecution and cover-up of some of the most heinous sexual crimes against children on a world-wide scale. Many authors seem to have the ability to ignore history, wholesale slaughter, theft, depravity and the plight of the victims. I cannot do this.

I have been told that those individuals who are very comfortable in their religious beliefs, and do not want to rock any religious boats, should not bother to read this book. According to some experts, these people will reject the material, they will deny it and they will become more resolute in their belief system. I know this is true, because not long ago, I was one of those people.

I held onto my religious comfort zone, with a strong dose of denial, for as long as I could. Denial is a very powerful force. But the combination of information, reason and curiosity are much more powerful. They are a relentless trio. They have been the primary elements for a research and writing effort that eventually became my sweat lodge.

"When you steal from one author, it's plagiarism; if you steal from many, it's research." Wilson Mizner (1876–1933)

1. INTRODUCTION

I hope that this book does not contribute to the deterioration of anyone's Christian faith, and I also hope that it does not influence anyone to completely abandon the Catholic religion. The entire book should be read before reaching any conclusions or passing judgement. The book may appear to have a destructive intent. However, the information that follows is structured to encourage the reader to raise questions concerning their religious beliefs and practices in an open, objective and constructive manner. One of my goals is to help motivate people to question the rules, dogma, practices and history of their religion. The terrible consequences of Roman Catholic Church actions requires probing questions, truthful answers and rigorous analysis. The motivating factors that promote behavior and attitudes that defile the Christ's teachings and insult a loving God must be examined. My intent is to disturb, but not to destroy. If some destruction is unavoidable, I hope that the overall effect is more like a jackhammer rather than a wrecking ball.

In Matthew 7: 7-8 and Luke 11: 9-10, Jesus strongly encourages us to "Seek—," and seeking is what we must do. What we "find" after we seek is often not pleasant or comforting. What I plan to do, in this book, is to question many of the claims made by the Roman Catholic Church since its inception and establishment as a state religion in the 4th century. I intend to discuss evidence that indicates many Roman Church claims are bogus, fraudulent, self-serving and even dangerous.

If all of the claims made by the Roman Catholic Church turn out to be false and fraudulent, does this mean that those who practice the Catholic faith are fraudulent, without God and with no true link to Jesus? Certainly not! In Matthew 18: 20, Jesus says, "For where two or three are gathered for My sake, there am I in the midst of them."

> "Do not think that love, in order to be genuine, has to be extraordinary. What we need, is to love without getting tired." Mother Theresa (1910–1997)

Jesus preached to, taught and healed the "multitudes." He did not discriminate against anyone who wanted to hear His message. All are welcome (John 6: 35, 37). In Matthew 28: 20, Jesus, gives us great comfort when He says "I am with you always, even unto the end of the world." In Luke 17: 21 and in the Gospel of Thomas, Jesus gives us more comfort and hope when He says, "the kingdom of God is within you." Jesus was not into church building. In Matthew 5: 17, Jesus says, "Do not think that I have come to abolish the Law or the Prophets. I have not come to destroy, but to fulfill." Jesus was not a legalist. He did not support or promote hierarchy. In Matthew 23: 1-39, Jesus admonishes the pompous hierarchy of His day. "Woe to you hypocrites, blind guides, fools, vipers—." Jesus provides more details on His feelings for hierarchy when He states in Matthew 19: 30 and Mark 10: 31 that "the first will be last, and the last first." But He is a friend to anyone who will listen. His basic commandment is loud and clear in Mark 12: 30-31, John 15: 17, John 13: 34-35 and Galatians 5: 14. We "must love one another," and get along with each other.

Truth, love, tolerance, integrity, fidelity and the beauty of Catholic belief have never been nurtured or welcomed in Rome. Love and spirituality appear to be absent in the Vatican. The true spiritual power of Catholicism is locked inside the hearts and souls of the Catholic laity. Without the Catholic faithful, the Vatican is nothing more than an impotent art museum and library. Jesus taught that the power of Christian faith comes from within us, not from above or outside the faithful or through a privileged hierarchical conduit.

No matter how confused, lost or troubled we become, Jesus gives us the same messages over and over again; "Seek. I am with you. God is in you. God loves you. I love you. Love one another. Arise and go your way, for your faith has saved you." Jesus did not designate any religious intermediary to interpret or validate the messages and instructions He gave us.

"How far it may be lawful and fitting to use falsehood as a medicine, and for the benefit of those who require to be deceived." Bishop Eusebius (~265–340 A.D.) From the 32nd Chapter of his 12th Book of Evangelical Preparation

In Matthew 7: 7-8 and Luke 11: 9-10, Jesus makes a statement similar to the following, "Seek and you shall find, knock and the door will be opened." However, Jesus did not promise that we would be comfortable with what we find, or that we would like what was on the other side of the door. In the Gospel of Thomas: 2, one of the translations indicates that Jesus said, "Let him who seeks continue seeking until he finds, when he finds he will become troubled, when he becomes troubled he will be astonished, and he will rule over the All." At this point I am far from "ruling" over anything. And, as a result of my seeking and finding, I am very troubled and astonished with the fraud, arrogance, tyranny and evil deeds willingly embraced by the religious entity that I followed and trusted for so many years.

Some of the material in this book is not going to be pleasant to read for those who strongly associate the Roman Catholic religion with their spirituality. For me, it appears that as a result of this effort of many years, I will have to remove the word "Roman" from my Roman Catholic religious tradition, and my spiritual practices. That is not going to be easy without being a little bit destructive.

Religion involves the observance, conformity and commitment to a specific corporate system of beliefs, dogma and actions administered and ruled by an earthly hierarchy. Spirituality is associated with a higher level of observance, devotion and commitment. It involves a personal relationship and communication with a more powerful earthly entity, or a divine Entity. It involves the attempt to follow sacred principles and teachings without allowing those principles and teachings to be distorted, corrupted or perverted by any person, organization or belief system. This is where religion and spirituality are often in conflict with each other.

"One day, history will record the madness of my Church." Fr. James Kavanaugh, from his book, *A Modern Priest Looks at His Outdated Church* (1968)

One critical question that must be asked is, "How does one preserve a reasonable part of Catholicism, and eliminate the corrupting influence of its Roman origins?" History and current events strongly indicate that the organized religion that baptized me does not conduct itself according to the moral code and integrity that Jesus promotes. The Roman Catholic Church does not follow the moral pathway or adhere to the high standards, it claims, have been entrusted to it's care.

It appears that the Roman Catholic Church has not developed and does not follow a healthy set of Christian values. The actions of this Church indicate that it is more focused on the "love of power," rather than the "power of love." This last remnant of a corrupt and brutal Roman Empire is exhibiting the symptoms of a structural and spiritual decay that has been ongoing since the reign of Constantine.

"There are people in the world so hungry, that God cannot appear to them except in the form of bread." Mahatma Gandhi (1869–1948)

2. DISCOVERING THE "VILLAIN" THAT JESUS DESCRIBES

I started working on this book at the age of 60, although the research effort began not long after my 30th birthday. For many years, my religious beliefs were constantly challenged by a close friend. His comments and questions, dating all the way back to high school, were components of the fuel that helped produce this fire.

Writing the first eight chapters was stressful. Initially, I was not sure why I felt compelled to write. As my writing effort evolved into a manuscript, working on the book became more and more unpleasant.

I had no real clear goal or focus. Much of my writing seemed scattered and pointless. I did not feel that I had anything constructive to offer. My writing effort seemed to be compulsive and obsessive. It did not appear to be a good use of my time and it did not appear to be appropriate. But, I could not stop writing.

Alice Flaherty has written an excellent book (*The Midnight Disease*, Houghton Mifflin (2004)) concerning the driving compulsion to write. The clinical term for this condition is hypergraphia. Hypergraphia can often be the result of disease, depression or repetitive shock. In my case, hypergraphia was a result of the repetitive shock, revulsion and horror that I felt as I studied the history of the Roman Catholic Church and compared that history with current attitudes, policies and behavior patterns of Roman Catholic hierarchy. As the results and initial conclusions of my research on the Roman Catholic religion developed, I went right into denial. But denial could not stifle my curiosity. Finally, the subjugation of denial by curiosity turned into objective inquiry. I had to search for "the truth;" no matter how much it hurt, and no matter what kind of discomfort it would bring to my life.

> "Speak the truth, and speak it ever, cost it what it will. For the wrong thing said is the wrong thing still." Anonymous, from the book *Alfred* (1983), by Al McDonald

As I investigated further, it became very obvious to me that the religion I had been following for many years, was not what it should be. Much of Roman Church history seemed to be a continuing horror story. It became clear that the Roman Catholic Church was established in the fourth century, as an extension of a corrupt and brutal Roman Empire, to solidify and unify the Roman political system. The Roman Church was the ultimate mix of religion and politics. It was a political entity cloaked in the vestments of a religion. The Name of Jesus was used, in a blasphemous way, as a bludgeon to destroy any belief system that deviated from Roman dogma and Roman rule. Millions of Christian men, women and children were hacked to death because their Christian beliefs did not fall in line with Rome's dictates. In the Roman Church, the Name of Jesus was valued, but the teachings of Jesus and His values were disregarded.

Based on its behavior, attitude and history; the Roman Catholic Church appears to be the villain Jesus describes in John 16: 2-3 and John 15: 21 when He says, "Yes, the hour is coming for everyone who kills you to think that he is offering worship to God. And those things they will do because they have not known the Father nor Me." "But all these things they will do to you for My Name's sake because they do not know Him Who sent Me."

For more than 16 years, I have been doing a considerable amount of research and development work, patenting, writing and lecturing in biomedicine and biophysics. A large part of this effort involves the use of electrotherapeutic techniques for the treatment of cancer, visual disease, connective tissue disease and neurological disease. This is an amazing therapeutic modality; simple, low cost and patient friendly. Electrotherapy has provided excellent benefits for many people with serious health problems. Working in the field of biomedicine makes me very happy. So I challenged myself, "Get off the soap box, man! Be happy! Do what you do best." But I could not get off that accursed soap box. I continued to write.

"It does not require many words to speak the truth." Chief Joseph, Nez Pierce, (1840–1904)

One day, a close friend gave me a little book to read. The book's title is *Alfred*. It was written by a bright, talented and funny man (Alfred McDonald); who I knew a long time ago. The book is a mix of thoughts and letters that Al McDonald wanted to write to people who were famous and not so famous.

Al McDonald's attitude, thoughts and spirituality gave me peace of mind, inspiration and direction. I am not sure how compatible *Isaiah's Leper* would be with Alfred's Roman Catholic beliefs. But, in one of the letters to a not-so-famous person, Alfred's words made me very glad that I continued writing. Alfred had a significant impact on me. His thoughts gave more meaning and direction to my quest. My attitude, outlook and life will not be the same, because of Alfred, and because of the not-so-famous person he addressed in his letter. The last time I saw or spoke to Al McDonald was over 35 years ago. He was not a close friend then. But he is a close friend now.

While writing the first seven chapters, I could feel a "hesitancy" that was the result of my Roman Catholic upbringing. One can object to or disagree with the thoughts and conclusions in the following chapters. But, the facts presented are well documented and available from many different sources, including Catholic libraries. I knew that I was on reasonably solid ground. What I was doing felt right, but it did not feel good.

As the writing effort continued, I began to feel much worse. The book was giving me big headaches. I was almost ready to put the entire manuscript in the paper shredder, and delete the book files in my computer. My mind was made up; *Isaiah's Leper* would never be released. I decided to finish chapter eight, and then, destroy the entire book. But, that did not happen. *Alfred* got to me at the bottom of the eighth.

"If the gods do evil, then they are not gods." Euripides, (480–406 B.C)

3. QUESTIONS AND CONCERNS THAT WILL NEVER GO AWAY

I was baptized a Roman Catholic. For some time, I was very comfortable with my religion. However, after investigating Roman Catholic Church history, dogma, practices, and the foundations of canon law; I began to realize that there were huge differences and conflicts between the church's religious structure, church teachings and my spirituality. As I evaluated the behavior, methods and record of the Roman Church; I began to realize that the traditional Roman Catholic religion, and my Christian spirituality, were not compatible.

Various stages of research and reconstruction have been in progress with respect to the structure of my own religious beliefs. As one might expect at any reconstruction site; this kind of activity involves a lot of demolition, chaos and noise. Reconstruction is often untidy and uncomfortable. Also, it can be dangerous.

I often think of the statement that appears in Fr. Andrew Greeley's book, *The Catholic Myth* (1); "In my heart, I am as Catholic as the pope, whether he thinks so or not." Greeley is right. In fact, in some ways, the dissenting Catholic faithful are far more Catholic (and Christian) than many popes and many others in the Roman Church hierarchy.

I have read large portions of the Bible, the Torah, certain Talmudic writings and the Koran. After recovering from the revulsion and horror that I felt when reading the content of those alleged "good books," I began to realize that all of them are important literary works that have been altered and manipulated. What seems to be behind all of the alteration and manipulation effort is the tribal motivation and logic to maintain power, establish political control through religious belief systems and justify a large number of very evil deeds.

"We do not want churches, because they will teach us to quarrel about God."
Chief Joseph, Nez Pierce (1840–1904)

Taking exception with 1 Timothy, the root of all evil is not money, or the love of money. The root of all evil, the "smoke of satan," is the combination of self deception and denial. Those two ugly relatives can be found lurking almost everywhere in the so-called "good books" or "sacred writings."

When I read portions of the Bible, Torah or Koran, I often have to put them down for awhile just to keep from becoming too repulsed or ill. Often, I smell "satan's smoke," and the smell is overwhelming. Religious deception and perversity increase as each of these "good books" is altered.

The "good books" all describe a bipolar disordered deity who approaches this world like a moody child, playing with poorly designed toys; smashing them with his fist when the toys do not please him. Does anyone realize how insulting and blasphemous this kind of description is to a merciful, just and loving God? Does anyone stop to think about the reasons why the dogma and actions of organized religion are often the root cause of so much evil and suffering in this world? And, why is God dragged in as a fully participating accomplice in this horrible mayhem?

The focus of this book is on, what many dissenting Catholics believe, are the authentic teachings of Jesus. In my own efforts to pull the teachings of Jesus out of the distortions, politics, power plays and agendas of man, I often ask the question, "Where does Jesus appear to be the hypocrite?" In Matthew 23, Jesus accuses the Pharisees of being fools. Then, in Matthew 5, He warns others not to call anyone a fool if they want to avoid the fire of hell. In Matthew 15, Mark 7 and 10 and Luke 18; Jesus repeats the Old Testament commandment "Honor your father and mother." And yet, in Mark 3, Luke 2 and John 2, Jesus seems rude and disrespectful toward his parents and family.

"We declare, we proclaim, we define that it is necessary for salvation that every human creature be subject to the Roman Pontiff." Pope Boniface VIII (1235–1303) from the 1302 Papal Bull *Unam Sanctam*

When I see discrepancies like these, I recognize them as the combined results of poor translation, blatant attempts to subjugate and outright fraudulent insertions. The discrepancies reflect the twisted manipulation and alteration of letters and Scripture implied in II Peter 2 and 3. Complaints concerning Scripture and document modifications are mentioned in letters from St. Faustus, St. Irenaeus and St. Dionysius. In fact, the Catholic Encyclopedia states that St. Dionysius referred to those who falsify the Scriptures as "apostles of the devil." Some of these "apostles of the devil" appear to have been in high places. In 382 A.D., St. Damasus I recalled (and apparently destroyed) certain sacred texts. Then, he allegedly asked St. Jerome to translate and revise Scripture, and force it to agree with Roman Church dogma. How often has this been done?

Combining the basic teachings of Jesus, with a belief in a just, merciful and loving God; there is much in the Bible that is obviously of the hand of man, having nothing to do with the Character or Word of God. In IV Kings 2: 23-24, forty two little boys call the prophet Elijah "baldy." Elijah curses them in the Name of the Lord. But the worst is yet to come. The Lord God sends two bears out of the forest and the beasts tear each of the boys apart—forty two little boys! In Acts 5: 1-11, St. Peter appears to be guilty of manslaughter. Annaias falls dead at Peter's feet after Peter scolds and berates the scheming Annaias, who cheated the apostles in a real estate transaction. But, Peter does not seem to be satisfied with manslaughter. Peter waits for the arrival of Sapphira, the conniving wife of Annaias. Peter scolds and berates Sapphira, and she falls dead at Peter's feet. Now we have first degree murder! In heaven's name, who had the audacity to insult God, the prophets and an apostle of Jesus like this? Who wrote these absurd fables, and what possessed them to do so?

"I am not concerned about all hell breaking loose, but that part of hell will break loose. If just part of hell breaks loose it will be much more difficult to detect." George Carlin

Yes, some of the material in these "good books" does appear to be insane. Some of it is outright blasphemy. But, between the lines of the self-serving dogmas, brutal deeds, corrupt logic and massive intolerance that appear in page after page of the Bible, Torah and Koran; every once and awhile I can see "Them." I hear Their words. God, Allah, Alaha, Jesus, Yeshua, Isa—They are All visible. They are not totally obscured by the smoke and haze of mankind's corrupt and fraudulent attempts to seize control and alter the basic teachings that are stored within our hearts and minds. When I see Them, my heart and soul are at peace; and I am filled with the energy of hope and love that form the foundation of my faith in Them.

"The devil can cite scripture for his purpose." William Shakespeare, (1564–1616), from The Merchant of Venice, Act 1, Scene III

4. WHAT ARE THE CONCERNS EXPRESSED BY PRIESTS, NUNS AND LAITY?

The foundation for this book is not completely based on my views, my concerns, my disappointments or my dissent concerning Roman Catholic Church history, teachings, attitudes, methods and conduct. The structural components of the book are forged by the fire of other Roman Catholics who have elected to voice their concerns, while remaining in the church. These dissenting priests, nuns and laity will not accept the hypocrisy and corruption that appears to run rampant in the church. But they have decided to continue their ministry and membership within a belief system that desperately needs them.

An interesting and impressive set of statements was made by a Roman Catholic woman in the March 8, 2002 issue of the National Catholic Reporter. She was commenting on the failure of Pope John Paul II to consider the wisdom of the laity or "lived reality," the church's loss of credibility due to its policies on birth control, the church's total folly regarding sex and the dysfunction in the Roman Catholic priesthood. She said, "I'm a returning Catholic after 15 years of separation from the church. Some of this (cover up of pedophilia in the priesthood) makes me angry enough to consider leaving once again. But I am aware that the Church has been around for over 2,000 years and there is great wisdom to be acquired by staying the course."

At the age of 75, Fr. Hans Küng, the Swiss theologian who disagrees with many elements of Roman Catholic Church dogma, expressed a wish to reconcile with the Vatican (National Catholic Reporter, pg. 9, April, 4, 2003). Fr. Küng has written volumes concerning avarice and hypocrisy in the Roman Catholic Church hierarchy and the lack of credibility in the papal claim of infallibility.

"*Trust, but verify.*" Russian proverb

Fr. Küng has written about the many broken lines in papal succession, papal and biblical forgeries, religious disputes being one of the primary contributing factors to war, the church's adherence to false teachings and the exclusivity of the Eucharist. However, in spite of his conscientious dissent, it appears that there is a desire on Fr. Küng's part to "stay the course." For years, I wondered, "Why?"

One must respect the desire on the part of dissenters to "stay the course" and maintain the practice of their religion as best as they can. But I still could not help wondering, "Why?" I read the comments made by Fr. Andrew Greeley on his INTERNET web site titled, "Why I'm Still a Catholic." I was critical of his comments, because I could not find one substantive reason for his desire to remain a Catholic. This is a priest who refers to Roman Catholic Church hierarchy as that gang of "corrupt thugs," "inept mean spirited careerists" and "the idiots who are running things." Fr. Greeley has been criticized for his dissent, disobedience and his earthy novels. And yet, there he is, against the wind, but "staying the course." There he is, holding on to what he feels still has tremendous value. What is it that Greeley, Küng and the Roman Catholic woman value?

A Los Angeles Times nation-wide survey of U.S. Catholic priests (October 20 and 21, 2002) indicated that 70% of the priests surveyed were "very satisfied" with their life as priests. Approximately 21% were "somewhat satisfied." The survey indicated that as far as the priests were concerned, the most important problems facing the Roman Catholic Church were the shortage of priests and problems with bishops and hierarchy. It would appear that the priests held similar views as many white collar workers would have with respect to their work environment and their management. However, the Los Angeles Times survey showed that there were very large discrepancies between the beliefs of the priests and Roman Catholic Church dogma, teachings and official church policies.

> "*Physics is not a religion. If it were, we'd have a much easier time raising money.*" Leon Lederman, Nobel Laureate

The November 1, 2002 issue of the National Catholic Reporter revealed that 40% of the Roman Catholic priests surveyed believed that "it is never a sin for married couples to use artificial birth control," 32% of the Roman Catholic priests surveyed stated that "it is seldom, or never, a sin for unmarried people to have sexual relations," 19% of the priests surveyed stated that "it is seldom, or never, a sin for a woman to get an abortion," 19% of the priests surveyed indicated that "it is never a sin to engage in homosexual behavior," and 17% believed that "it is never a sin to take one's own life if suffering from a debilitating disease." The National Catholic Reporter stated that these views, from a sample of American Roman Catholic priests, match the opinions of lay Catholics "to reveal a priesthood and a laity less inclined than ever to define a good Catholic in terms that agree with church norms."

An examination of the Letters to the Editor in the National Catholic Reporter (NCR) between 2001 to 2003 indicates that approximately 50% of the letters from priests and nuns were highly supportive and unquestioning with respect to church policies and methods. The other 50% showed significant dissent, even to the point of mutiny and revulsion. The following comments are a sample of those taken from priests who expressed concern, revulsion, dissent and outrage.

"The division of Christians into cleric and lay is a longstanding practice that should be abolished—first, in our thinking and speaking, and eventually from cannon law." (NCR, March 29, 2002)

"We join other Catholics in calling for the resignation and punishment for those bishops whose oversight failed." (NCR, November 15, 2002)

"I can only assume that Pope John Paul II is completely out of touch with the workings of the Holy Spirit." (NCR, April 5, 2002)

"I would have made a good pope." Richard M. Nixon (1913–1994)

"The church, in other words, the people of God, finally give notice that they are reclaiming the legitimate Spirit-filled power that has always belonged to them." (NCR, April 11, 2003)

"Patently, something is terribly amiss in the structure and formation of the Catholic clergy for our day that is not apparent in other Christian denominations." (NCR, December 13 and 20, 2002)

"Faith is not to be put in a human person whatever their status in the church; not in an institution, be it parish, diocese or church as organized society. Our faith must be firmly fixed in the person of Jesus Christ." (NCR, September 27, 2002)

"While the bishops' moral authority and credibility are crumbling around them, when are they going to wake up to reality and acknowledge their major role in damaging the church we love by irresponsible and perhaps criminal behavior? They have perpetrated an evil menace through silence, cover-ups and hush monies. It is beyond me how these bishops can live with themselves, let alone sleep at night. But then again, they have had years of practice by closing their eyes to criminal behavior." (NCR, April 26, 2002)

"Many of the problems of Catholicism are the result of its adamantine obsession with controlling other people's lives; particularly their sex lives. It is amazing that a church, whose social teaching is intellectually so advanced, can have ideas on sex that are naïve, one-dimensional and positively preadolescent. Isn't it time we all grew up, read a book published after 1545 and used our brains?" (NCR, April 11, 2003)

"For credibility, the church needs to practice what it preaches." (NCR, August 1, 2003)

"Give me chastity and continence, but not yet." St. Augustine (354–430 A.D.)

"In the face of dwindling resources, bishops are seeking to protect their own despotic status—the seemingly brazen indifference demonstrated by the hierarchy to the welfare of the pedophile victims and their families is the same indifference many priests have experienced for years." (NCR, May 24, 2002)

"The desire to preserve the status quo, to which the pedophilia problem must be traced, is much more evident. Spokesmen for the bishops twist away in childish fashion from facing a fact plain to all. Married Protestant ministers do not have the pedophilia problem that we have." (NCR, April 25, 2003)

"Many lay Catholics are becoming adults in their interactions with church authorities. When that happens, the priest himself is challenged to become an adult." (NCR, "Priestly Identity in Church's Time of Darkness," April 25, 2003)

"One problem is the utter inadequacy of the oversight provided by Rome, largely through a self-reporting system. To think that the pope and a few offices in Rome can adequately provide such oversight, not only for American bishops, but for all bishops of the world, is to believe in Santa Claus. This (pedophile cover-up scandal) was a disaster waiting to happen, with many preliminary warnings. We can no longer afford to hide or bury the sins of the church. The gifts of God need to be adequately recognized and employed in the governance of the church. In this time of disaster, I believe it will be the laity who save the church, not the bishops or priests." (NCR, August 1, 2003)

"The church will need Vatican III to restore and implement what the second council began. What a price the church has paid for the total allegiance and nearly blind obedience to Rome and the pope!" (NCR, May 17, 2002)

"Love is a flaming friendship." Variation of a quote from English bishop and theologian, Jeremy Taylor (1613–1667)

Auxiliary Bishop Joseph M. Sullivan of Brooklyn had the courage to address the sins of the Roman Catholic Church (NCR, May 30, 2003) when he said that "the church must end the culture of secrecy and give a greater role to the laity in finances and the selection of bishops and priests." In his dealings with Pope Pius IX, a quotation from Cardinal John Henry Newman (NCR, October, 25, 2002) revealed his true feelings about papal abuses and the arrogance of church hierarchy when he said, "It is not good for a pope to live 20 years. It is an anomaly and bears no good fruit; he becomes a god, has no one to contradict him, does not know facts and does cruel things without meaning it."

Many nuns have expressed their displeasure in ways that are somewhat different from most dissenting or concerned priests. Many nuns tend to be less diplomatic, more focused and they describe specifics related to church problems and church sins in greater clarity than some of their priestly counterparts. The following comments from nuns, to the NCR Letters to the Editor, provide a few examples.

"The church's ecclesiastical culture is riddled with rot and hypocrisy. Priests who preach chastity while enjoying mistresses on the side, priests who lead double lives while preaching honesty, priests who pilfer from the collection plate while condemning thievery, priests who live in luxury while urging concern for the poor, priests who abuse power and indulge in basic cruelty while quoting St. Paul on chastity, the crushing of dissent and enforcement—. I feel sorry for the good priests. But the truth of the matter is, they have known! Why haven't they spoken out? What forces have been and are still at work in the church culture to keep all this hidden?" (NCR, April 26, 2002)

"Don't let the abusers off the hook!" (NCR, February 28, 2003)

"A people that values its privileges above its principles soon loses both."
Dwight D. Eisenhower (1890–1969)

"This business of having a tribunal of clerics to investigate and bring to trial an accused priest is like making a rule that only members of the Mafia can investigate and bring to trial another Mafia member. Where is the justice? Where is the accountability? Where are the sanctions?" (NCR, November 29, 2002)

"We as the church today face so much tragedy, sin, criminal behavior and abuse of power and wealth by clergy and hierarchy. I would suggest for their prayerful consideration the words of Jesus as recorded in Matthew 23: 24-25: Blind guides! You strain out the gnat and swallow the camel. Woe to you Scribes and Pharisees, you frauds! You cleanse the outside of the cup and dish and leave the inside filled with loot and lust!" (NCR, November, 2002)

There are many insightful comments from the laity. They appear to have a better understanding of what is fact and what is fiction than church hierarchy realize. Laity often have an excellent understanding of church history, the actual teachings of Jesus, the obscene games played with cannon law and the legal system and the impact of the church's culture of secrecy and corruption. An informed and educated laity often makes it difficult for the church hierarchy to maintain its posture of a dictatorship and its cloak of secrecy. The following comments are from dissenting or concerned Catholic laity.

"Tragically, the real causes for the depth of the present crisis are an improper use of authority and the pathology of secrecy, silence and deceit that begin in the highest offices of the church and filters down." (NCR, May 24, 2002)

"Reform always comes from the bottom, just as certainly as corruption always comes from the top." (NCR, February 14, 2003)

"Castles made of sand fall into the sea, eventually." Jimi Hendrix (1942–1970)

"A Catholic priest recently suggested to me that the secrecy and intrigue of the current scandal bespeak the hierarchy's desperate attempt to hide not only terrible deeds but also the spiritual vacuum of the inner sanctum. Could it be that the marrow of the church's bones has dried up because it does not consistently open itself to the wisdom of its laity? A church hierarchy that lives in fear of change, controls its membership through the inculcation of blind obedience and limits access to theological knowledge simply cannot be a healthy institution." (NCR, January 17, 2003)

"If human cloning is morally unacceptable, why does the church continue to clone bishops?" (NCR, March 28, 2003)

"The early church was born in times of kings and princes and its operational structure reflected this form of governing. Today's church operates in democratic societies, a fact that should be reflected in its everyday operation. If Christ came upon this earth today, in America, do you think He would toss aside the freedoms we hold dear, and establish a medieval style church? Not likely!" (NCR, March 28, 2003)

"Every cardinal makes a vow to the pope, never to reveal to anyone whatever has been confided in secret and the revelation of which could cause damage or dishonor to the Holy Church. This vow corrupts the cardinal's obligation to obey civil laws that apply to everyone including laws prohibiting false statements and obstruction of justice." (NCR, July 18, 2003)

"Public criticism of political figures (who do not support Catholic dogma and teachings) is a clear attempt at coercion. But coercion of this sort is repeatedly denounced by the Vatican II document, Declaration on Religious Freedom." (NCR, July 18, 2003)

"Religion and politics are an incendiary combination." Margot Patterson

"Let me see if I can get this straight. The Vatican is questioning sexual abuse policy because it might violate due process and rights of priests? Yet, as a Catholic theologian, I know case after case of lay Catholics who have been dismissed from their jobs in Catholic institutions without a whisper of due process or any hearing at all. I know other theologians who have been silenced after secret hearings held in the Vatican, at which the theologians under suspicion were not even permitted to know the charges made against them. Suddenly, when priests are involved, the Vatican is concerned about human rights." (NCR, November 1, 2002; Also see NCR, August 13, 2004, pg. 12)

"The vow of obedience taken by our priests has become a vow to sin if their superiors demand it." (NCR, May 10, 2002)

"I firmly believe that a vocation is a grace given by the Spirit. And if Catholics are not flocking to the seminaries, monasteries and convents of our day, it is because the Spirit is not calling them in great numbers to do so, in order to build a completely different church than we have known heretofore." (NCR, August 1, 2003)

"This is a church that talks a lot to the faithful about their sexuality, and yet has obvious problems dealing with clerical sexual abuse and cover ups in America, Africa and elsewhere." (NCR, February 14, 2003)

"Now let me see if I have this straight. Women who procure abortions are excommunicated. Women who are ordained are excommunicated. Priest pedophiles are not. What's wrong with this picture?" (NCR, February 14, 2003)

"Now, now my good man. This is no time for making enemies." Voltaire (1694–1778), on his deathbed, in response to a priest asking that he renounce Satan

"Many of our bishops, acting out of fear, more concerned with protecting the institution than protecting innocent victims, allowed those victims to be sacrificed on the altar of institutional idolatry, which is choosing the self over God." (NCR, February 14, 2003)

"Despite the delusional and amoral hierarchy, Catholics for the most part continue to blindly go to the church and give deference to the morally bankrupt church hierarchy. What kind of faith and example does this provide our children? Certainly not the faith that Christ sought to give us." (February 28, 2003)

Based on the comments made by concerned, dissenting and outraged Roman Catholic priests, nuns and laity; we can assemble a number of terms and statements they have used to describe the condition of the church, church attitudes and church methods. Then, in some of the following chapters we can use those terms and statements as guides, to ask strategically important questions concerning the status and validity of specific demands imposed by Catholic dogma.

Several of the comments from the priests, nuns and laity point to the lack of spirituality in the Roman Catholic hierarchy. They indicate that certain elements of Roman Catholic church attitude, teachings and behavior are not worthy representations of the teachings of Jesus Christ. They describe the Roman Church as abandoning God, being an unhealthy (sick) institution, not truthful, secretive, sinful, criminal, violating due process, hypocritical and full of double standards, driven by avarice, bearing no good fruit, fearful of change, degraded by thievery, perpetrating an evil menace, deceitful and despotic.

Do these terms and observations provided by concerned priests, nuns and laity truly represent characteristics associated with certain parts of the Roman Catholic Church? If they are a reasonably true representation, what is our obligation and what is our response?

"You can observe a lot by watching." Yogi Berra

Many of these comments from priests, nuns and laity are damning. They have acknowledged and condemned the corruption, criminal behavior, depravity, hypocrisy and immorality of the Roman Catholic Church hierarchy and its practices. And yet, many of the people who make these statements continue their ministry, their religious duties and their membership in the Catholic Church. These dissenting Catholics are "staying the course." Why? What encourages them to, "hold on?" What is it that Fr. Greeley, Fr. Küng and the dissenting Roman Catholic laity value?

In his book, *The Catholic Myth, The Behavior and Beliefs of American Catholics*, Fr. Andrew Greeley gives the results of his research on why people hold on to their Catholic faith (1). Fr. Greeley indicates that the degree of attachment to the rituals, symbols and community life of the local parish is a primary component of the "loyalty" that Catholic laity have to "stay the course" and not leave the Catholic Church. This loyalty has been an anchor for many Roman Catholics. This kind of loyalty enables many American Catholics to remain practicing Catholics. And yet, they can express their opposition and disgust with a church whose leadership endorses moral and political stands that are contrary to one's convictions, that are often in violation of civil law and are often contrary to the teachings of Jesus.

Fr. Greeley's assessment appears to be a blend of his work as a sociologist, his personal convictions and his personal needs. I have my own convictions and needs, and I know why I have not totally abandoned a portion of my own Catholic traditions. I value attending church services with others, because I firmly believe that where two or more are gathered (or joined) in the Name of Jesus, to commemorate His life and death, I believe that He is there. Jesus is present, not because of any church structure or authority. He is present because of the people who gather for His sake, and in His Name.

"All things are connected. Whatever befalls the earth, befalls the Children of the earth." Chief Seattle, Suquamish (1786–1866)

I value attending church services with others because I want to show my support for them and my support for their hope, their love and their faith. It is my way of demonstrating that I believe they all have God within them, and around them. It is the way I show my love and respect for them. In church, I feel the presence of Jesus of Nazareth, through the presence, faith and hope of the congregation. The priest or bishop are nothing more than fellow participants. The true source of power for any religious gathering is through the participants, not from a self-serving and dictatorial corporate religious intermediary. Communion is the sharing of a symbolic meal with others. From the standpoint of spirituality, we are connected. The pagan inspired transubstantiation dogma is not necessary. Luke 17: 21, the Gospel of Thomas and Matthew 28:20 state that the kingdom of God, Jesus and the Holy Spirit are already with us, within us and around us. I do not need to take communion to bring God, Jesus and the Holy Spirit into my body. A guarantee has been given that They are already there. However, I do need to take communion as a renewal with other Christian believers, to show my support for them, and to "do this in commemoration of Him."

Why do the origins and behavior of the Roman Catholic Church seem to be the antithesis of what Jesus represented and taught? What would have happened to Christianity, and Catholicism, without the balance and principles introduced by the Protestant Reformation? If Martin Luther had not risked being burned at the stake, it is difficult to imagine the kind of organized religious monster that would have evolved. Luther did not eliminate the corruption and depravity that he saw in the Roman Church and its hierarchy. But he did succeed in slowing down and mitigating the process of religious degradation that was the trademark of the Roman influence. Thank God for the Protestant Reformation! It saved Catholicism from itself, and it saved Christianity from a total Roman infestation.

"I cannot and will not recant anything, for to go against conscience is neither right nor safe. Here I stand, I can do no other, so help me God." Martin Luther (1483–1546), allegedly stated at the Diet of Worms, Germany on April 18, 1521

In his January 30, 2004 National Catholic Reporter article on religious institutions, Fenton Johnson states that, "for all their warts, religious institutions preserve collective wisdom." I strongly disagree with Johnson's statement. Hierarchical elements within the Roman Catholic religious institution have burned more books than they have written. Once they burned the books, they often burned the people who wrote the books or read them. The Roman Church, and other religious institutions, are famous for their efforts to suppress and withhold information and "collective wisdom" from many cultures and groups inside and outside of Christianity. Religious institutions do not have a reputation for preserving or protecting collective wisdom.

Further on, in his National Catholic Reporter article, Johnson states that "Christianity was one of the first to popularize religion as a means for all people (rich or poor, male or female) to live a whole and meaningful life. In his teachings, Jesus draws upon Greek philosophy as well as the Jewish commitment to equality, firmly grounded in tolerance, mercy and charity." This is why I have not completely severed my ties with the Catholic Church. It has incredible potential. And some day, it could become what it appears to be.

As a true Christian Church, teaching and following the principles that Jesus taught, the Catholic Church could become a Christ-inspired positive influence. It is possible that the Catholic Church could become the entity that Johnson describes. But, in order for this to happen; a massive amount of reconciliation, reconstruction and re-thinking will have to be done by this religious entity. Fr. James Kavanaugh and Fr. Hans Küng have expressed the opinion that Roman Catholicism, as a monolithic structure, is disappearing (2, 3). Since its inception in the early fourth century, the Roman Catholic Church has been corrupted by Roman attitudes, tradition and methods. The Roman Church has rejected the basic teachings of Jesus, betraying Him in ways that are much more horrible and criminal than the final recorded actions of Judas Iscariot.

"Forgive your enemies, but never forget their names." John F. Kennedy (1917–1963)

5. WHAT IS THE FUNDAMENTAL FLAW IN MOST ORGANIZED RELIGIONS?

In processes of religious reconstruction that involve the "evolution" of knowledge and thought, some beliefs and dogma will always end up failing to meet the standards of truth and credibility. This happens in science, economics and business all the time. Religion is not immune to this kind of failure. Every religion, every belief system and every social system possesses structural components that have flaws, serious errors and inconsistencies. As an example, the Roman Catholic Church used to burn people at the stake for professing scientific beliefs that, later on, were verified and accepted.

To establish authority and control, organized religions often use brutal statements, teachings and interpretations; invoking God's approval (and active participation); such as "—exterminate the last of them, leaving none alive, doomed to destruction, receiving no mercy, but to be exterminated as the Lord had commanded" (Bible, Joshua 6: 2-21 and 11: 6-9), or "Even the best of gentiles (*Goim*) should all be killed" (Talmud, Soferim 15, Rule 10) or "We will cast terror into the hearts of those who disbelieve—" (Koran, Surah III, 151) or "—Allah's curse is on the unbelievers" (Koran, Surah II, 89). If God, Ala-ha or Allah are loving, merciful and just; the claim that these words and teachings are Their desires and Their commands would be highly contrary, evil, destructive and the highest level of blasphemy.

The Roman Catholic Church appears to have engaged in its own unique forms of destruction and blasphemy. How do we explain the logic behind the butchery of the Crusades and the Inquisition? How do we explain the Dark Ages (roughly from 476 A.D. to approximately 1,000 A.D.) "when religion ruled the Western world." Some historians describe the beginning of the Dark Ages as "the night everyone went to bed smart, and the next morning, they woke up stupid."

> *"Only two things are infinite, the universe and human stupidity, and I'm not sure of the former."* Albert Einstein (1879–1955)

During the Dark Ages, progress in science, medicine and sanitation was tossed aside, and a motionless state of decay ruled in the regions under Roman Church influence for over 500 years. This was the period when Roman Catholicism was dominated by fundamentalist ideals and ideas, to an extreme. The essence of the Dark Ages was it's "despair of life on earth" (4).

Examples of the effects of fundamentalism in the early Roman Church would include the brutal murder of the philosopher Hypatia, in 415–416 A.D., by followers of St. Cyril. According to St. Cyril, Hypatia apparently deserved the treatment she received because "she was an iniquitous female who had presumed, against God's commandments, to teach men" (5). With that kind of perverse reasoning, almost every female teacher would have to be put to death.

The Church's 16th and 17th century suppression of the heliocentric (sun-centered) model of the solar system, proposed by Copernicus and Galileo, could be considered the result of religious fundamentalism fueled by intolerance. At that time, Roman Catholic Church doctrine stated that the earth was the center of the universe (geocentric). In 1616, the sun-centered system of Nicolaus Copernicus was considered heresy. Copernicus's *De Revolutionibus Orbium Coelestium* was placed in the Church's Index of Forbidden Books (even though Copernicus apparently tried to soften his position with the Church by dedicating his book to the pope). The Inquisition's willingness to burn heretics at the stake and the condemnation of Copernicus's book served as an effective weapon and implied threat for the Church in its attempts to silence Galileo in 1632–1633 (6).

The butchery and evil of the Crusades against the Albigensians, Muslims, Jews and others (11th–13th centuries) and the Inquisition (12th–early 19th centuries) are perverse effects of religious Roman Church fundamentalism. Remnants of the Crusades continue, and can be identified with the 1990's strife in Bosnia and Kosovo (7).

"*I don't bend.*" Pope John Paul II (1920–2005)

The philosophy, attitude and methods of the Inquisition still live on in the Roman Church's Holy Office of the Inquisition, or it's more sanitized title, Congregation for the Doctrine of the Faith.

There is an interesting contrast that can be made between Roman Catholicism and Islam. Approximately 100 years after the Roman Catholic Church was officially established as the state religion by the Emperor, Theodosius, the Dark Ages occurred. However, 100 years after Islam was established, the Arab culture enjoyed the "Golden Age of Islam," and it flourished from the mid-8th to mid-13th centuries (8, 9). What was the basic difference between these two religious beliefs? What produced such a massively destructive result with the initial Roman Church influence, compared with the more constructive and civilized result that occurred when Islam was first introduced? Some would answer that, once placed in power, the Roman Church revealed its oppressive and corrupt tendencies, and it's fundamentalist attitude, almost immediately. After defending itself against the intolerance and brutality of the Roman Church and papal extravagances, Islam appears to have initially promoted a much healthier and more civilized attitude and philosophy. But, something changed. Historians point to a rise in Islamic fundamentalism in the 11th century (10).

There are many concerns about the destructive effects of Islamic fundamentalism (8, 11). Do some Islamic fundamentalist attitudes and dogmas exhibit the same destructive and corrupting influences as the Roman Church possessed when it had so much power? During the Golden Age, the Arab culture provided a massive influx of knowledge in science, mathematics, economics, language, art, poetry and social ideals (8, 9, 12). The Arab people are members of a highly creative culture. Did the decline of the Golden Age of Islam occur when fundamentalist ideas and ideals undermined the tremendous potential and breadth of Arab creativity and vision?

"Reason is not to be trusted too much. Faith and mysticism are safer guides."
St. Bonaventure (1221–1274)

Anyone who attempts to answer this question must keep in mind that, from the late 11th century to the 16th century, the Arabs had their hands full. Starting in 1099; the insanity, brutality and fundamentalist ideals of the papal inspired Christian Crusades were forced upon the Arab population. If that was not enough, the Arabs had to face massacre and subjugation by two Mongol hordes, and they had to suffer two invasions of the Black Death (12). That level of interference and destruction would appear to be more than enough to bring a decline to any culture. However, in order to answer this question concerning reasons for the decline, truthfully, we must face reality. We cannot allow ourselves to drift into the usual state of self deception and denial that often accompanies answers concerning the effects of religious fundamentalist ideas and ideals.

In his book, *The Story of Civilization* (10), Will Durant writes, "The Mohammedan conquest of India was probably the bloodiest story in history. It is a discouraging tale—." What Durant is referring to is the incredibly savage Holocaust that the Hindu people suffered at the hands of various Islamic invaders from the 11th through the 14th centuries. During this time, some of the Muslim military leaders considered it meritorious to kill at least 100,000 Hindu men, women and children every year. From Arab accounts of these activities, one could estimate that more than 1.5 million Hindus were slain. If the early 1900's slaughter of 1.5 million Armenian Christians, by Turkish Muslims is included, it would appear that certain segments of Islam may be responsible for several Holocausts involving the murder of more than 3 million people. This was done while invoking the sacred Name of Allah, the Compassionate, Merciful and Beneficent One. Would a Compassionate, Merciful and Beneficent Sustainer and Lord of the World approve of holocausts, honor killings and genocide? In the Islamic belief system, would Allah's Apostle, Isa (Jesus) approve? What are the effects on a culture that promotes or tolerates fundamentalist dogma that results in holocaust activity?

"Denial ain't just a river in Egypt." Mark Twain (1835–1910)

Before answering questions concerning religiously induced cultural declines, we should examine the Bible's account of the Holocaust in the Land of Canaan, and the possible effects of this effort on the Israelites who participated; allegedly with God's support, blessing and active participation. Approximately 14 pages of the Old Testament and Torah reveal some interesting statistics. In a few passages of Joshua, Numbers and Deuteronomy; the Israelites destroyed over 40 cities (full of bad people) and more than 20 tribes of these same bad people. At an average of 20,000 individuals per city or region, and adding another 600,000 Canaanite soldiers slain in battle, these pages indicate a slaughter of almost 1.5 million people in, and near, the Land of Canaan by the Israelites. Were all of the people in the Land of Canaan that bad?

Many of the Bible or Torah passages start or end with phrases similar to the following: "—and God (or the Lord) commanded to be put to the sword—," followed by: "—leaving no survivors" (Joshua 10: 37), or "—putting to the sword all living creatures in the city: men and women, young and old as well as ox and sheep and ass" (Joshua 6: 20), or "—exterminate the last of them, leaving none alive," doomed to destruction, receiving no mercy, but to be exterminated as the Lord had commanded (Joshua 11: 14-15). Is this the legacy of a just and merciful God of love?

I have listened to several Rabbis explain the previous paragraph. The explanation goes something like this: "Well, you see, the Israelite conquest of the Land of Canaan was a form of 'cleansing' or 'purification,' by the Israelites so that they could take their rightful place in a land that was held by a corrupt and Godless people." What I find horrifying about this statement is that it reflects the same type of attitudes and recommendations that appear in Adolf Hitler's book, *Mein Kampf*, and many Nazi rabble rousing speeches that were made, to promote the "final solution," the destruction of the Jewish race.

"Self-deception is infinitely expandable." John Leo

Would a God, who loves his children, support a genocidal philosophy? Would a merciful and just God promote, set up and enthusiastically participate in Holocausts, ethnic "cleansing" and "purification" activities? Again, before answering any questions, we might consider the 13th century Holocaust of Southern France, directed by the Roman Catholic Church. Over a 30 year time period, it is estimated that more than one million people, judged to be in conflict with official Church teachings, were slaughtered by papal supported military forces (5). This long-term event has been identified as the first European genocide (13). Many of these Crusades and genocide activities were justified by the use of Luke's Gospel (Luke 19: 11-27), where Jesus uses a parable and is alleged to have ended it with the statement, "But as for these my enemies, who did not want me to be king over them, bring them here and slay them in my presence." In truth, the authenticity of Jesus making this kind of statement is in doubt. Jesus was (is) a smart and politically astute man. He would have known that a "slay them in my presence" statement would serve as a dangerous weapon for any zealot or fundamentalist. Jesus said, "all are welcome." Jesus wants us to "love one another," "turn the other cheek" and refrain from "scandalizing the little ones." Would this same Jesus endorse the papal supported pillage, rape, plunder and murder of more than one million people?

In various parts of Jewish, Arab and Christian history; each culture has gone through a "God has abandoned us" period, and each culture came up with various reasons (some, very self-serving) for this perceived abandonment. However, it appears that the organized religions of these cultures are the ones that have abandoned Allah, God, Jesus and Their Apostles with numerous distortions and perversions of the original intent and teachings of a Merciful, All knowing, Almighty and Beneficent Lord (14, 15).

"We want to be people of faith, not people drugged on the narcotic of religion. We are not able to endure the mental lobotomy that one suspects is the fate of those who project themselves as the unquestioning religious citizens of our age." Episcopal Bishop J. S. Spong, from his book, *Why Christianity Must Change or Die* (1998)

One of the more dangerous aspects of religion involves the tendency for different groups of people to consider themselves "chosen." Christianity, Judaism, Islam, Hindu, Native American, etc. all have statements or claims identifying themselves as "the chosen ones." This aspect of considering one's culture as "chosen" has been the source of a massive amount of cyclical butchery, death and destruction for more than 4000 years. "We are the chosen ones," "God is on our side, and "ethnic cleansing for purification" are the self deceptive slogans and ideals that promote large amounts of evil, slaughter and depravity.

In fact, there is one characteristic that often stands out with any hard core fundamentalist "chosen ones" religious mentality or attitude. This characteristic involves how and what those belief systems attack. Within reason, members of any belief system can criticize or attack another belief system's answers or conclusions. However, when critics attack an honest question, that is a sure sign that they are trapped in the desperation of a corrupt, intolerant and self-serving belief system.

Certain statements provide subtle and effective ways to attack questions. As an example, the following statement has been used for centuries by organized religions to suppress inquiry, debate, curiosity and doubt: "Your questions are indicative of your lack of faith." This particular statement or admonishment, in response to valid questions, serves as a hiding place for many belief systems that are inadequate, corrupt, self serving and outdated. This statement is the battle cry of a belief system, or organization, that has something to hide and cannot withstand scrutiny. The Roman Catholic Church is just one of those religions that has been very defensive in the face of intellectual maturity and scrutiny, to the point of suppressing curiosity. Many Roman Catholics (and clerics) consider honest questions and critical analysis of Roman Catholic affairs as evidence of disloyalty (16).

"Those who dance are considered insane by those who cannot hear the music." George Carlin

Many clerics and popes have attempted to avoid scrutiny by declaring that the Church, with it's divinely inspired papal head, is the conduit by which Christ's grace flows from the hierarchy into humanity (see *De Concordantia Catholica* or, On Catholic Concord). However, some of the real reasons for this "conduit" theory are obvious. In 1449, Jacob of Juttorborg wrote that the claim of papal supremacy is only a shield to hide behind, so that Roman Church prelates could shelter themselves from reform (17).

Whenever religious belief systems state their "facts," ask for their sources. When a religious system is secretive, determine what the reasons might be for the secretive attitude. People and organizations do not hide what is appropriate, they hide what is inappropriate.

Some Catholic theologians have stated that Catholicism can no longer be a matter of belief in formulas, but must be based more on reality. Certain dogmas of the Roman Catholic religion are now forced upon the faithful because many of these dogmas no longer have enough intellectual support to be accepted on the basis of faith (16, 18). In his book, *The Ascent of Man* (19), Jacob Bronowski states that you cannot possibly maintain an informed integrity "if you let other people run the world for you while you yourself continue to live out of a ragbag of morals that come from past beliefs."

From Matthew 7: 7-8 and Luke 11: 9-10, Jesus says: "Seek," but what the Roman Catholic Church really appears to be afraid of comes next: "and ye shall find—." The Roman Catholic Church, and other Christian religions, are going to have to face the fact that intolerance, suppression, mindless censorship and conformity are incompatible with religious, spiritual and intellectual development. It is becoming obvious that these attitudes and practices have even failed to promote the maintenance of healthy moral standards and ethical conduct for a significant portion of the Roman Catholic Church's own clerical ranks and hierarchy.

"*Curiosity is the root of heresy.*" Pope (St.) Gregory the Great (540–604)

If our past has any significant meaning for us, the historical record of the behavior of almost all organized religions and belief systems guarantees a cycle of violence and butchery that will continue unabated, as long as each (or any) of those religions maintains their attitudes of arrogance, intolerance and suppression. The Holocausts that accompany these attitudes repeat themselves. If allowed to continue, they will become more awesome and sophisticated, involving larger numbers of victims and larger geographical areas.

The magnitudes of pre-1800 Holocausts committed by Christians, Muslims and the Israelites required 30 to 100 years to accomplish with swords, spears and crude firearms. Using a combination of perverted Christianity, Roman Empire symbolism, logistics, incineration and chemical technology; Nazi Germany was able to slaughter more than four times the usual number of Holocaust victims in one tenth the time required by it's predecessors. A conservative estimate of the numbers of Jews murdered in the Nazi Holocaust is approximately 6 million (20). Using a lower tech approach for genocidal policies (starvation), Joseph Stalin was able to exterminate 10 million to 20 million of those he viewed as being uncooperative or undesirable (21, 22).

Considering the potential of nuclear and biological weapons, the term "Holocaust" no longer seems appropriate. Extinction might be a more applicable term. In time, the threat of Total Extinction, resulting from the actions of religious fundamentalism, may have a much higher probability than a Total Extinction Event resulting from volcanic activity or the earth's interaction with a wandering asteroid.

> *"Kill them all, for God knows his own."* the answer given by Pope Innocent III's papal legate, Arnaud in 1209 at Béziers, when asked how to distinguish Catholic from heretic. The estimated numbers of men, women and children slain range from 6,000 to more than 60,000. This was done in an attempt to kill a relatively small number of alleged Cathar heretics (5, 13). The authors of the Catholic Encyclopedia deny that this statement was ever made by the papal legate, but they do not deny the slaughter.

So, what are the reasons for the decline of the Golden Age of Islam or the decay of Roman Catholicism, or the struggle faced by Judaism? Why the decline? Why the decay? Why the struggle? Some would answer that all three of these organized religions have essentially abandoned the principles, values and teachings of their Originators. All three appear to have fallen victim to their own denial and self deceptive tendencies; justifying their intolerance, arrogance, atrocities and exaggerated fundamentalist attitudes. All three appear to have become the antithesis of what their Creators represent. At the peak of their success, these religions appear to have abandoned the true principles and spirit of their God. They may now all be suffering from the consequences of emphasizing and perverting external religion, at the expense of their own internal spirituality and integrity.

Fr. Hans Küng has pointed out that the Roman system, Orthodox traditionalism and Protestant fundamentalism will disappear, simply because they are not of the essence of Christianity (23). Since, most of the current organized religions appear to have exaggerated their fundamentalist attitudes, lost their spiritual values and lost their "essence;" Fr. Küng's forecast for Christianity would appear to be applicable to all major religions. And, it would appear that the world might be a better place to live, without the influence of any of these religious entities, in their present form.

In conclusion, it is becoming evident that one of the more dangerous and destructive aspects of religious beliefs involves any set of characteristics that promote fundamentalism, intolerance and the arrogance of different groups that consider themselves "chosen." These are the self serving and self-deceptive ideas and ideals that have contributed to a considerable amount of holocaust activity and genocide. There will be no end to the cycle of madness and slaughter until this "chosen ones" propaganda is ripped out of every belief system.

"Adapt or perish." Charles Darwin (1809–1882) and H.G. Wells (1866–1946)

6. DOES THE ROMAN CATHOLIC CHURCH FOLLOW THE BASIC TEACHINGS OF JESUS?

Let's give Jesus, the Man, a few thoughts. Imagine His last moment on that brutal cross. This is not a nice sanitary crucifixion as displayed in paintings and on the statues we see in church. Jesus suffered an incredible series of beatings, tortures and violations. He is drenched in sweat, dirt, blood, urine, diarrhea and vomit. His eyes are wild and unfocused. He cries out, His head bobs from side to side, His body heaves one last time. And then, He dies. The earth darkens, time stands still and nothing moves. The last thing Jesus hears is the sound of a gentle breeze. Two thousand years later, standing in your kitchen, you hear the pleasant sound of a gentle breeze. All of a sudden, Jesus appears before you, naked, dirty, beaten bloody and full of wounds. Both of you just stand there, looking at each other in stunned silence.

Jesus looks confused: "Where am I? How did I get here? Who are you? What happened to Me?" But, what eventually takes over in your close encounter with each other is curiosity. Once Jesus realizes that He is almost 2,000 years ahead of the time of His death, He is going to want a lot of information from you. "Do you know Me? Did I make a difference?" Your reply might be something like: "Did You make a difference? Did You make a difference?! Holy shit, Man! You are the Difference!"

And of course, at that moment, you feel very embarrassed and start to apologize to Jesus for your crude speech. Jesus puts you at ease by saying, "Don't worry about it, I am not offended. Many of My friends were fishermen. They could not talk, walk, eat or catch fish without shouting out their large assortment of highly creative obscenities." You both laugh. What a moment! Both of you have so much to ask of each other. And of course, Jesus wants to hear it all. "Friend, My name is Yeshua, but you may call Me Jesus if you like. First, I must wash Myself. And to do so, it appears I will need a lot of water. Then, please, tell Me everything I hunger to know."

"*I believe because it is absurd.*" Tertullian (155–220 A.D.)

As Jesus finishes bathing, you don't know where to begin your dialogue. You feel panic, realizing that you have forgotten so much! You find a warm bathrobe and a pair of slippers for Him. The only slippers you have are the ones purchased from the novelty store, with big fake bear claws. Jesus puts them on. He laughs and says, "How do I look?" You reply, "It is You Jesus! It is really you! Now, how do we begin? Where do we begin?" Searching your memory, you introduce a variety of subjects; the New Testament, St. Paul, early Christian martyrs, St. Francis of Assisi, the missionary work, Mother Theresa, cathedrals, Pope John XXIII. Jesus interrupts, "What is a pope?" You try your best to explain the structure of the Roman Catholic Church. You explain what led up to the use of the papal title in the late fourth or fifth century, along with the fifth century declaration that the bishop of Rome was the highest ranking bishop. Jesus interrupts again, "Bishop of Rome!? Roman Catholic Church!? What happened to the community of Jerusalem? What happened to James, their leader? What happened to the other communities that were led by many good men and women disciples? This is all very confusing!"

Jesus has that "deer in headlights" look about Him. You can see a lack of recognition, on His part. You realize that there is a difference concerning what you are describing, and what He expected to hear. Now you start to get nervous. How do you describe to Him the formation of a legalistic and secretive male-dominated church, that abandoned and eventually persecuted its Jewish roots, abandoned its vital community spirit, abandoned its simple structure and threw away any significant female influence?

Looking directly into the confused and dazed eyes of Jesus, how do you explain that, by mixing Christian beliefs and pagan mythology, a Roman Catholic Church was formed. How do you tell Him that this religion was empowered under the Roman Emperors Constantine, Theodosias and Justinian; and officially incorporated as a state religion by the Roman Emperor Theodosius?

> *"If you are going through hell, keep going."* Sir Winston Churchill (1874–1965)

Jesus taught: "Love one another," "All are welcome," "Do not scandalize the little ones," "turn the other cheek." How do you tell Him that under these Roman Emperors, tens of thousands, maybe a million, of the Christ's early followers were put to the sword, in His Name, because their beliefs did not match the teachings of the Roman Catholic Church regarding Jesus as the exclusive Son of God rather than the adopted Son of God?

For a moment something else grabs your attention. "Uh, Jesus, You are bleeding from Your nose and ear. I'll get You something for that." You give Jesus a box of gauze pads, a cold wet towel and another clean bathrobe. Again, He is genuinely appreciative. "Thank you friend. The Romans are a relentless bunch, with their continuous hitting, kicking and lashing. I am having trouble hearing with this bleeding ear; and those barbarians broke My nose." A broken nose? For a moment, you are puzzled by this discrepancy with John 19: 36.

You look at His blood stained bathrobe, you look at the tissue missing from His left ear and other parts of His body, "Jesus, I think those barbarians broke your eardrum. You need medical attention." Jesus shakes His head. "No! No! I will be all right. I don't know how much time I have with you. We need to talk. Please, continue."

Watching Jesus nurse a bloody nose and a bleeding ear, you are also aware of the incredible numbers of lash marks, spear and knife wounds and stripped flesh on His body. How do you tell Him? Your initial feeling of excitement and pride has gone. The news is only going to get worse from here on. You begin to feel slightly nauseated.

How do you tell this beaten and battered Jesus about the holocaust of the Crusades, the horrors of the 600 year Inquisition, the St. Bartholomew's Day Massacre, the 30 Years War, the Vatican bank, the accounts in the Cayman Islands used to loot insurance companies. How do you explain the millions of people murdered in His Name?

"A friend is a gift you give yourself." Robert Louis Stevenson (1850–1894)

How do you rationalize the Roman Church's support for weapons of war in Catholic Countries like Croatia and Argentina? How do you discuss the Roman Church's massive cover-up and protection of pedophile priests and bishops on an international scale; all done "to "protect the image of Holy Mother Church?" That is just a small sample of what you are going to have to tell Jesus. How will He feel, and what will He say?

You look at Jesus very carefully, and your curiosity takes over, "Jesus, You are not what I expected—." You have difficulty finishing your statement. Jesus, looks concerned, and a little hurt. "My friend, is it My speech? I know I talk too fast. And I often change directions, from one subject to another. Is it the way I look? I apologize for My appearance. Roman punishment can be a bit stressful on the body and mind. Tell Me, is it because I am small of stature, or not of your race? Tell Me My friend, have I offended or disappointed you?"

You become overwhelmed with emotion. With tears streaming from your eyes, you softly touch His bruised and bleeding shoulder. "Jesus, You could never disappoint me or offend me. But, I am very worried. I just don't want to disappoint or offend You. We have a lot to talk about, and most of it will not be pleasant."

Jesus, notices the food on your kitchen counter top. "That smells good!" You quickly recover and smile at Him. "I just purchased sandwiches and beer from a Jewish delicatessen. It is as kosher as we are going to get. Are You hungry?" Jesus replies, "Oh yes! Let's eat! And while we eat, please tell Me everything! I can live with the truth. And eventually, I will respond to the truth in My own way."

For a moment, you gaze at this small Semite man, with Hamite blood, this small Man, Who casts a giant shadow—. You think to yourself, "No one will ever believe me." But it does not matter, because Jesus has shown how much He believes in you.

"Do not confuse motion with progress." Paul Wichtendahl

Based on his teachings, Jesus supports the belief that God did not give us intelligence and reason to just put them on display. Jesus wants us to "Seek." He wants us to think. Faith in Jesus does not impose blind obedience to an organization that has a documented history of corruption, intolerance, avarice, persecution, war crimes, hypocrisy, brutality and murder. These characteristics are well documented and can even be found in the Catholic Encyclopedia, Catholic newspapers and subpoenaed Catholic documents. Jesus rejected and condemned this kind of organization many times, and in many ways.

1. Corruption: *The desire to save image, maintain power and protect the wealth of the Catholic Church has motivated a massive amount of cover up activity all over the world with respect to problems involving pedophilia and other violations of sexual behavior. Two thirds of U.S. bishops participated in the attempts to conceal sexual crimes when they clandestinely transferred pedophile priests to unsuspecting parishes. The 2004 U.S. nationwide survey on sex abuse among Catholic clergy indicates that, since 1950, about 4% of U.S. Roman Catholic priests have been accused of molesting minors (24). At most, only one half of the incidents are ever reported. And, recognizing that the molestation of minors is only part of the sexual behavior cover up activity within the Roman Catholic Church, it appears that approximately 10% of Roman Catholic clergy have been involved in some facet of the sexual misbehavior scandals. The percentage is probably much higher in other parts of the world. The sexual misbehavior problem goes right up to the level of the pope's advisors (25).*

2. Intolerance and Persecution: *The Crusades of Popes Urban II, Alexander III and Innocent III exceeded the bounds of depravity, imposing a harsh symphony of brutality, genocide and extermination against uncooperative Christians, Jews and Muslims. Over a thirty year period, a large part of the population of Southern France was decimated by the Crusades against the Cathars. The effects of these crusades against other Christians can still be seen in Southern France. During this time period, estimates are that approximately one million people were slaughtered by the Roman Church (5, 23). More than 100,000 Jews were slain and, during a thirty year time frame, over 200,000 Muslims were killed by marauding Crusaders.*

"Nothing is possible unless one will commands, and all others obey." Adolf Hitler (1889–1945)

3. **Avarice:** *From the 11th century on, the statement, "Everything is for sale in the Vatican" has been a common joke and an embarrassment (4). Rather than being bogged down with a lot of excuse making for the excesses of the early Roman Church, let's look at some recent examples, where hierarchy behaviors may be more difficult to defend, because memories and documentation are fresh.*

   Beginning in 1998, Msgr. Emilio Colagiovanni, a former judge on the Vatican's central appellate court and legal advisor to the pope, engaged in a scheme with Martin Frenkel, a Connecticut business man, to defraud U.S. insurance companies of more than $200 M. Apparently, the Vatican bank cooperated with this fraud by transferring $50 M through a bogus foundation, and finally into the Vatican's St. Francis of Assisi Foundation. Once the scheme was uncovered, the Vatican denied having any association with the St. Francis of Assisi Foundation (26). However, significant transaction and consulting payments were apparently made to the Vatican bank and to Msgr. Colagiovanni. The Vatican bank apparently agreed to serve as the money launder in exchange for a ten percent cut of the millions that would be looted from U.S. insurance companies (27).

   The Bishop of the Rockville Centre (Long Island) diocese apparently displaced a group of nuns from their home, and cancelled a $1.1 M home care program for indigent and mentally ill people on Long Island; while spending significant sums of money for his own residence (described by many as palatial) in 2002 (28). In 1999, prosecutors in Southern Naples made recommendations that the cardinal of Naples be sent to trial for loan-sharking (29).

   One of the "sleaziest" frauds in many years occurred in the 1980's, involving the Vatican Bank's responsibility and participation in the fraudulent bankruptcy of the Banco Ambrosio; and removal of substantial amounts of money from other banks. Some of the 830 million lira that disappeared from the Banco Ambrosio, apparently found its way into, and out of, the Vatican Bank under the direction of the Head of the Vatican Bank, Archbishop Paul Marcinkus (30). Many murders, attempted suicides and arrests followed this debacle (31). The Vatican bank apparently received kick backs from the illegal transfer of funds to take control of various banks and front companies, to purchase Exocet missiles for Argentina in the

   > "I do not run the country, but I do run Chicago. I am only answerable to God and to Rome." Cardinal John Cody, Archbishop of Chicago (1907–1982), in response to federal grand jury subpoenas (31) to examine his financial records while facing multiple charges of pocketing and illegally diverting church funds.

Falklands war, to hide illegally purchased grossly overvalued shares in the Banco Ambrosio and to provide large loans to shell companies and Vatican owned front companies in Panama, Luxemborg and Liechtenstein (27, 31).

4. War Crimes: *The war crime record of the Roman Catholic Church reveals a substantial amount of hypocrisy and highly corrupt double standards in Church activities involving the Vatican's clandestine and substantial support of world-wide warfare and bloodshed, for causes that serve Roman Catholic interests.*

The number of demands, pleas, suggestions, submissions and plans for peace in Iraq, Bosnia, Afghanistan, Central and South America, etc. that have been expressed or proposed by Roman Catholic hierarchy are impressive. Equally impressive, and disturbing, are the previously mentioned well-documented efforts by the early Roman Catholic Church; in waging war to murder those who have been accused of dissent, heresy or being uncooperative with Roman Catholicism. But this church sponsored activity did not stop with the Crusades, the 30 Years War, the holocaust in Southern France or the butchery in the New Americas.

There is ample evidence of recent efforts by the Roman Catholic Church to provide money for arms purchases (27, 31) for Catholic countries (Argentina and Croatia) and militant Catholic groups like the Irish Republican Army. The Indian Express (Nov. 22, 1999) and several South African newspapers reported that the Vatican secretly sent the Croatian government $40 M worth of bearer bonds to purchase weapons for the Bosnian War. This activity occurred during a time when the Vatican was promoting peace and understanding in Bosnia. The scheme was revealed in a Johannesburg court during the trial of former chemical warfare chief Wouter Basson. This plot was exposed as the result of an effort by some of the participants to skim approximately $1.4 M for drug deals.

But one of the most well documented, and disturbing, accounts of the complicity of the Roman Catholic Church in war crimes is its WWII support of the massacre of more than 500,000 Orthodox Serbians by the Croatian Ustashi; and, with bayonets at their throats, the forced conversion to Catholicism of more than 244,000 Serbs by the Ustashi (32). Many Ustashi units were led by Franciscan priests; such as Fr. Bozidar Bralow (the machine gunner), Fr. Miroslav Filipovic (the executioner of the Jasenovoe death camp, with its crematoriums), Fr. Zvonko Brekalo, Fr.

"*Glory be to God, our gratitude to Adolf Hitler, and infinite loyalty to Ante Pavelić.*" From the Official Croatian Catholic Newspaper, April 28, 1941 (32)

Zvonko Lipovac and Fr. Josef Culina (Ustashi who all aided Fr. Filipovic in the Jasenovoe slaughter, Brekalo was decorated for his deeds), Fr. Grga Blazevitch (assistant to the commandant at the Bosanski-Novi concentration camp) and Fr. G. Casimir, who supervised the butchery at Glina (27, 31)). Apparently, the ethnic cleansing being done by the Croatian Ustashi was so brutal, that hardened Nazi SS officers reported to Hitler that "the Ustashi have gone raving mad (27)."

But, with respect to the Roman Catholic Church participation, the after-effects of this madness never ends. Money obtained from the mass forced conversions of Orthodox Serbians was apparently collected and deposited into Franciscan accounts at the Vatican bank. The Vatican was given a percentage of the money and loot that was collected from converted Serbians and slaughtered Serbians, Jews and Gypsies. Arrested for war crimes, Archbishop Stepinac of Croatia was rescued from prosecution by the Vatican and the U.S. Pope Pius XII did not make one statement of censure against the Ustashi. The reports of Croatian and Ustashi atrocities were dismissed as Communist anti-Catholic propaganda. In 1998, Pope John Paul II traveled to Croatia to announce the beatification of Archbishop Stepinac (27). Like St. Cyril, if Stepinac is canonized, the Roman Catholic Church will be accused of adding another saint to its roster, who was so bad that, "hell is not hot enough to hold him."

5. Hypocrisy: *When sued for pedophile behavior and protection of pedophile priests, or accused of obstruction of justice; some bishops have resorted to the theological argument that central to the church's faith is its belief in the power of redemption and the forgiveness of sins (33, 34, 35). They want to be absolved from their apparent criminal acts. Roman Catholic hierarchy have been very quick to promote understanding, tolerance and forgiveness when it comes to their own sins and heinous crimes. But they seem to have swept aside any thought of understanding, tolerance, forgiveness and redemption for the Orthodox Christians and Cathars slaughtered in the various Crusades, the Christians accused of heresy during the 600 year Inquisition, Protestant Christians during the 30 Years War, Catholics who engage in dissent and divorced Catholics.*

Quoting Luke 23: 34, Luke 24: 46-47, Luke 17: 3-4, Matthew 6: 14-15, Matthew 18: 35 and Mark 11: 24-26; in their attempts to be forgiven, the Catholic hierarchy

"Theology is so notorious as a dreary, futile word game, an endless shuffling of the counters of all-ness and not-ness, that one may forget its value and its necessity." H. Muller (1905–1980)

continually avoid one of the items that Jesus attaches to the act of forgiveness; and that is true repentance. Roman Catholic hierarchy seldom show any significant levels of repentance, even after being caught engaging in criminal activity. Their attitudes and Vatican attitudes on the treatment of sexual crimes and sins by Catholic clergy are stated in the 1962 document, Crimen Sollicitationis, and the proceedings fall under the category of pontifical secrecy. Many civil attorneys have pointed to the document as evidence of the Roman Catholic Church's obstruction of justice (35). By maintaining a secretive posture in an attempt to obstruct justice, proper repentance cannot be achieved by Catholic hierarchy who are guilty of criminal activity and sin.

6. **Brutality and Murder:** *The murder of Hypatia in 415–416 A.D. by St. Cyril's followers, and Cyril's excuse for that murder, offer a hint of how far an organized religion will go to suppress dissent. Thousands of Christians who did not believe "the right way" were put to the sword by the Emperor Constantine, Theodosius and Justinian (23, 36). In 1209, thousands of Christian's were slaughtered in the city of Béziers to kill a relatively small number of heretics (5, 13). When Italian city states organized revolts against tribute payments and papal control, Pope Gregory XI sent his papal legate, Cardinal Robert of Geneva, and a group of mercenaries to seize control. In 1377, during a three day murderous rampage in the town of Cesena, young and old were put to the sword. Women were raped and children were held for ransom. Approximately 2,500 to 5,000 Christians were slaughtered by the representatives of Pope Gregory XI (5).*

The barbarity, depravity and looting associated with the Crusades and Inquisition were a source of control and riches for a church and papacy that would stop at nothing to increase its base of power and enhance its wealth. The aftermath of the Crusades extended right into WWII and the Bosnian War. The atrocities committed by Roman Catholics (Croatians) and Orthodox Christians (Serbians) against each other, and the wholesale slaughter that they promote, are characteristics of most organized religion conflicts. The Roman Catholic Church's participation can often be easily identified by the unique and exaggerated levels of brutality and slaughter that occur in specific events during these conflicts. As an exercise; starting from its beginnings in the fourth century, add up the numbers of Muslims, Jews, and members of various Christian belief systems that have been killed by, or for, the Roman Church. Which group has the highest number killed? The answer will be a surprise for most people.

"What is truth?" **Pontius Pilate** (John 18: 38)

7. **Violating the basic teachings of Jesus:** *Jesus has essentially one prime commandment, and that commandment is that we "love one another." (John 15: 17). He makes a similar statement in John 13: 34-35. In another passage, Jesus gives us two commandments. Jesus instructs us to love the Lord and love our and neighbor as ourselves because "On these two commandments depend the whole Law the Prophets (Matthew 22: 40). Jesus even states that we should love our enemies (Luke 6: 35)! What part of "Love one another" does the Roman Catholic Church have a problem understanding? To believe in the teachings of Jesus, one would have to reject, condemn and regard as anathema, all of the Roman Catholic Church attitudes, teachings, behavior and policies that contributed to the events described in items 1 through 6.*

In Matthew 18: 6, Jesus teaches, "But he that shall scandalize one of these little ones that believe in me, it were better for him that a millstone should be hanged about his neck, and that he should be drowned in the depths of the sea." With two thirds of the U.S. Catholic bishops having participated in the protection and transfer of over four thousand pedophile priests, and with a significant amount of the records of these activities kept secret in Vatican files, there are many Roman Catholic hierarchy who should be carrying a millstone in deep water. In Matthew 18: 7-9, Jesus recommends that we "cut off" and "cast from thee" any thing that scandalizes us. Jesus is not simply referring to physical parts of our bodies in these passages. Using symbolism, he is referring more to our religion and our attitudes. In other words, "if your religion or your attitude scandalizes thee, cut it off and cast it from thee." In Luke 12: 1, Jesus says, "Beware of the leaven of the Pharisees, which is hypocrisy." This is a clear warning from Jesus to be aware of the consequences of the corruption that exists in any hierarchy.

The Roman Catholic Church is highly secretive, especially with respect to its crimes and sins. But in Luke 12: 2-3, Jesus says, "Everything that is hidden will be found out, and every secret will be known. Whatever you say in the dark will be heard when it is day. Whatever you whisper in a closed room will be shouted from the housetops." The insular and secretive structure supported by Roman Church hierarchy has no place in any religion that promotes Jesus. Jesus teaches accountability and transparency. These are concepts that are totally at odds with the way the Roman Catholic Church is structured and the way it operates.

"Nothing is as it seems." **Unknown**

At this point, St. Thomas Aquinas, a highly respected Roman Catholic Church Doctor, would encourage us to start asking some hard questions. In his day, St. Thomas's inquiries were considered very troublesome and dangerous. So, one of those troublesome and dangerous questions has to be asked; "Does the Roman Catholic Church follow the basic teachings of Jesus?" We would probably have to reach the same conclusions as those stated by Fr. James Kavanaugh, Fr. Hans Küng and Episcopal Bishop John Spong. Based on the hard evidence in items 1–7, the answer has to be; "Generally, No!" The Roman Catholic Church appears to support teachings, attitudes and policies that are often the antithesis of what Jesus of Nazareth taught, encouraged, promoted and supported. Jesus openly rejected much of what the Roman Catholic Church does, supports and represents.

"When Jesus stretched his arms wide on the cross, he was saying, 'I love you this much.'" Rick Warren, minister

7. IS THE ROMAN CATHOLIC CHURCH THE ONE TRUE CHURCH ESTABLISHED BY JESUS?

Some scholars insist that the designation "Catholic Church" was used at the beginning of the second century and the term "Roman Catholic" was introduced by Protestant reformers. However, the Roman Catholic Church origins and establishment are well documented. The word "Roman" is very important because this church was established as a legal entity by the Roman Emperor Constantine in 313 A.D. (Edict of Milan), and eventually given the status of a ruling religious entity (state religion) by the Roman Emperor Theodosius in the latter part of the fourth century. During the reign of these Roman Emperors, Roman Catholicism became an interesting and colorful blend of modified Christian and Pagan doctrine, beliefs and ritual. The Roman Church was formed more than 250 years after the death of Christ, and its belief system became significantly different compared to the wide range of various Christian beliefs that flourished during the previous time period. In fact, many Christians who did not go along with the official Roman state version of Catholicism were put to the sword—in some cases; every man, woman and child of that particular uncooperative group (23).

Roman Empire Catholicism was initiated, fabricated, debated and decreed during the time period of the Battle of the Milvian Bridge (312 A.D.), the Edict of Milan (313 A.D.), the Council of Nicea (325 A.D.) and beyond. One of the significant structural elements of this religion incorporated a significant component of Roman rule—fear. Essentially, "obey the rules, or die." Roman Catholicism did not exist before the fourth century. This Roman state religion has no believable or credible link to Jesus, the Christ; who was "crucified, died and buried" approximately 250 years earlier.

> "The church must not be afraid of historical truth—Historical truth must be sought severely, with impartiality, and in its entirety." Pope John Paul II, from *Tertio Millenio Adveniente*

From information written in the New Testament and the Catholic Encyclopedia, and as predicted in Isaiah 2: 2-3, the religious entity that Jesus founded was the Jewish Jerusalem community; led by St. James, the brother of Jesus. This was the religious community and group of people that St. Paul often debated (II Corinthians 11: 4-6), scolded (Galatians 2: 11-15) and ignored (Galatians 1: 16-19). Some scholars refer to St. Paul as "the first heretic because of his many apparent insults against and disagreements with the original Jerusalem community of the Christ's apostles and followers. In fact, Paul exalts himself and his "labor" over some of the apostles (I Corinthians 15: 10, II Corinthians 11: 3-6), and he claims a special relationship, knowledge of and bond with Jesus that no one else seems to have (Galatians 1: 10-12, Ephesians 3: 1-4).

St. Paul appears to have been a serious concern for St. James with respect to Paul's tendency to turn his back on Jewish law and custom (Acts 21: 21). And St. Paul was the most significant influence with respect to the rapid break between modern Christianity, the original Christian community and early Christian Jewish roots. Paul establishes his position as an apostle, essentially a 12th apostle who "sets himself apart" and replaces Judas (I Corinthians 1: 1, Romans 1: 1). However, Paul is promoted and exalted even further. The book of Acts and some of Paul's Epistles appear to be setting Paul up as the main founder and authority of the Gentile church (Galatians 2: 7-9)—the Pauline version of Christianity (Acts 9: 3-6, I Corinthians 11: 23-34, Acts 9: 15-16, Galatians 1: 15-17, Galatians 2: 20-21). In fact, in Galatians 2: 7 and 9, Paul has gospel teaching authority over the Gentiles and Peter has authority over the "circumcised," or the Jewish Christians (a group that made Peter fearful of mixing with Gentiles, as indicated in Galatians 2: 12). Galatians 2 eliminates the possibility that St. Peter could be considered the head (or original pope) for any major segment of Christianity today. St. Paul's claim is that, as revealed by the Christ, Paul was the authority over the Gentile Christians; which would include the Roman Catholic Church.

"Can't we all just—get along?" Rodney King

Is the Roman Catholic Church the one true church founded by Christ? The evidence indicates that the answer to that question would have to be, "Absolutely not," for quite a few reasons. In Peter's Confession, the statement allegedly made by Jesus, making Peter the "rock of My church" (Matthew 16: 17-19) does not appear in the account of Peter's Confession in Luke 9: 18-21 or Mark 8: 27-30. This may well be another one of the many "touch ups" or "additions" that often appear in the Bible. It is doubtful that Jesus ever made the "rock of My church" statement to Peter, a man who Jesus refers to as a "satan" just a few lines later, in Mark 8: 32-33 and Matthew 16: 22-23.

St. Paul's writings in Galatians 2 give Peter and the other apostles an authority over the Jewish Christian community. St. Paul reveals that both he and Barnabas have been given authority over the Gentile Christian community. So the Roman Catholic Church's legacy claims, as originating through St. Peter, automatically throw out its claims to legitimacy as the "one true church" of Jesus Christ. St. James, St. Peter and the other apostles could provide a strong link to Jesus, and an appropriate legacy for the Christian faith, through the original Jerusalem community. However, with Roman Catholicism's strong ties to a Roman Empire birthplace and a Pauline Christian doctrine; Roman Catholicism has no direct credible link to Jesus Christ and his remaining 11 apostles. That link can only be forged through the Jewish tradition and the original Jerusalem community.

There is a 240 year gap in time between the establishment of the Roman Catholic Church (a hybridization of Christianity and Paganism) and the remnants of the original Jerusalem community of Jesus and St. James. St. Paul was responsible for a considerable amount of the doctrinal and organizational gap between the original followers of Jesus and the Roman Catholic Church.

> "We should always be disposed to believe that which appears to us to be white is really black, if the hierarchy of the church so decides." St. Ignatius Loyola (1491–1556)

There are a number of very interesting hints in Galatians 1: 14-24 concerning St. Paul's disregard for the original Jerusalem community leadership, and his impressions of St. Peter. Paul establishes himself as being "very special." He says, "I advanced in Judaism above many of my contemporaries (verse 14)" and "God called me, through His grace (verse 15) to reveal His Son in me, that I might preach Him among the Gentiles immediately, without taking counsel with flesh and blood (verse 16)—and they glorified God in me (verse 24)." Also, in verses 16 and 17, Paul indicates that he ignored the Jerusalem community, St. James and the other apostles and went out on his own. However, Paul does eventually visit St. Peter and remained with Peter for fifteen days (verse 18). Although he saw St. James (verse 19), Paul spends his time with Peter. There is probably a very good reason why Paul concentrated on Peter and ignored the rest of the Jerusalem community.

What is interesting about Galatians 1: 16 and 24 is that Paul makes a statement that parallels the more general statement for all of us, from the Gospel of Thomas 3; that God and the Son of God are in him.

In dealing with the Jerusalem community, obviously, Paul did not have much influence with St. James. James was very strong willed and uncompromising. James was more like a zealot. St. Peter was a big strong man, a bully, but more pliable. As Peter's recorded behavior has indicated, Peter was more easily compromised. Being a bully himself, St. Paul knew how to manipulate this kind of personality. St. Paul always seems to keep St. Peter somewhat on the defensive. Paul admonishes Peter in some places (Galatians 2: 11-14) and he indicates that Peter and James may not be the pillars of leadership that they should be (Galatians 2:9).

"There is nothing so easy as by sheer volubility to deceive a common crowd or an uneducated congregation, such most admire what they fail to understand." St. Jerome (347–419 A.D.), Epistle LII to Nepotian

Occasionally, Paul gives Peter a small compliment; in some cases, Paul mentions Peter's position of leadership and relationship with Jesus (Galatians 2: 7-8, I Corinthians 15: 5). Paul works on Peter for some time (fifteen days) in Galatians 1: 18. Peter is Paul's best candidate for conversion to Paul's way of thinking. Paul had bitter disagreements with Barnabas (Acts 15: 36-41). St. James also seems to distance himself from some of Paul's statements. In James 2: 14-22, St. James appears to be upset by St. Paul's methods and teachings, especially Paul's emphasis on the importance of faith over good works for salvation.

Paul knows the weak links in the Jerusalem community. Paul seems to know that if he can get anyone in the Jerusalem leadership to bend, it will be Peter. And, to a degree, it works! In II Peter 3: 15, Peter compliments and exalts "our beloved brother Paul, according to the wisdom given to him." There are a number of writings that make St. Peter and St. Paul look like they are in agreement. And yet, Peter indicates that he is not completely won over by Paul's persuasive personality and Paul's writings. In verse 16, St. Peter states, "As also in all his (Paul's) epistles, speaking in them of those things, in which are some things hard to understand, which untaught and unstable people twist to their own destruction, as they do also the rest of Scriptures." In his own way, Peter appears to be concerned about Paul's tendencies to contradict himself; at times to yield, at other times to strike back, to be non-discriminatory at some times and very discriminatory at others. Peter also gives us the first hint of the fraudulent activity that was occurring, at that time, with Scripture.

There are a number of additional questions that we might ask. One of those inquiries concerns the Epistles of Peter (I Peter and II Peter). The question must be asked, "Who wrote I Peter and II Peter?" It certainly could not have been St. Peter. As indicated in Acts 4: 13, Peter and John were "uneducated and untrained." Using the words "uneducated and untrained" is a more gentle way to describe Peter (along with John) as being illiterate. So, who wrote Peter's Epistles?

"Nearly all men die of their medicines, not of their diseases." Molière (1622–1672)

It would appear that the legitimacy, integrity and credibility of the Catholic Church was, initially, highly compromised when it separated itself from its Jewish roots, hybridized itself with a diluted form of Christian theology and Pagan ritual and tried to pass itself off as being the lawful and rightful organizational descendant of Jesus of Nazareth and his remaining apostles. At that point, the Roman Catholic Church exceeded St. Paul's claims to a unique relationship with Jesus and his schismatic activity that promoted the original separation from St. James, the apostles and the community of the Christ. Jesus, St. James and St. Peter would have been appalled at the idolatry, corruption, politics, legalism and savage butchery that characterized the Roman Church as it evolved. The Roman Catholic Church, and many other organized Christian religions, could never flourish if they were truly forced to operate under the teachings and example of Jesus.

As Fr. Hans Küng has indicated, the final crushing blow to the Roman Church's credibility and integrity occurred when Pope Pius IX decreed something that a number of popes, clerics and saints considered to be myth, madness and evil; the doctrine of papal infallibility (3).

The evidence indicates that the Roman Church significantly modified the teachings, roots and traditions originally promoted and established by Jesus. The New Testament describes the initial efforts of St. Paul to separate Gentile Christianity and the original Jewish Christian community of Jesus. Several centuries later, the huge political weight of the Roman Church enhanced and completed this separation. Many early Christians regarded the symbols, dogma, traditions and methods of this Roman hybrid of Christianity and Paganism as hideous, blasphemous and murderous. And, true to form, the Roman Church used a murder weapon as their symbol—the cross.

"You shall know the truth and the truth shall make you free, but first it will make you miserable." Carl Rogers (1902–1987)

8. IS THE PAPAL LINE UNBROKEN AND INFALLIBLE (EX CATHEDRA)?

This question cannot be properly addressed without some initial thoughts concerning the relationships between Jesus of Nazareth and the hierarchical structure and function of the Roman Catholic Church. In Matthew 23: 1-33, Jesus says "Do not call anyone on earth your father," "And do not be called teachers," "But he who is greatest among you shall be your servant," "And whoever exalts himself shall be humbled," "But woe to you scribes and Pharisees, hypocrites—blind guides, who strain out a gnat and swallow a camel—fools—full of extortion and self-indulgence—Serpents, brood of vipers! How can you escape the condemnation of hell?" Jesus cannot be accused of "beating around the bush" or being subtle here. Jesus was not just addressing the scribes and Pharisees of his time. He was condemning the hypocrisy, lust for power, greed, perversity and malevolence of hierarchy for all time to come. Jesus never intended to form an institution like the hybridized Roman Catholic state religion. Jesus provided a very strong set of statements demonstrating to us that He did not want to be associated with a religious governing dictatorship that seeks absolute authority, power, legal might and wealth.

For instance, in Matthew 15: 21-28, Jesus appears to be in a bad mood when the Canaanite woman begs Him to cure her sick daughter. Jesus seems to be a bit rude to her, "It is not good to take the children's bread and throw it to the dogs." The followers of Jesus are also rude, "Send her away, for she cries out after us." But the woman persists, "Yes Lord, yet even the little dogs eat the crumbs which fall from the master's table."

"Caminante, no hay camino, se hace camino al andar. Traveler, there is no path. Paths are made by walking." Antonio Machado (1875–1939)

Reading this passage in Matthew 15 very carefully, realizing the meaning of "little dogs," recognizing the Canaanite woman's unselfish love and devotion, recognizing her respectful and faith filled persistence; the warm Heart of Jesus returned, and His reply was one driven by His high regard and respect for her, and His ability to recognize the important lesson that she was teaching. "Oh woman, great is your faith! Let it be to you as you desire." And her daughter was healed from that very hour.

Jesus seems to have had a bad day, and He was surrounded by a group of rude and inconsiderate disciples who appear to have been getting on each other's nerves. Who teaches the lesson here? The teacher is not Jesus. The teacher is the Canaanite woman. Jesus and His disciples learned much from the Gentile woman on that day. Being a sensitive man, Jesus probably felt some sadness with the way this humble, yet noble, Canaanite woman was being treated. Like many of us who are temporarily blinded by our irritations, Jesus and His disciples were slow to recognize the precious gifts they were receiving from this persistent and patient mother. Her gifts were her faith, her love and her persistence. Her faith, love and persistence demonstrated to Jesus and His disciples that God's love, salvation and the entire legacy from Jesus are not limited to particular groups or persons. They belong to all who have faith in the teachings of Jesus. This simple truth is verified in many of Jesus of Nazareth's statements including John 3: 16, Luke 17: 19 and Luke 7: 50. "Woman, great is your faith—."

I think of this Canaanite woman often. I admire her spunk, her dedication and her diplomacy. It is hard to ignore the wisdom that was evident in her pleas and replies. Her spiritual power rules over any hierarchical authority or papal claim. Her faith is what nourishes Christianity and gives it life. Without the likes of her, there is no Church. I believe that she made a big impression on Jesus, and I believe that Jesus thought about her throughout the rest of His life.

"Live simply, so that others may simply live." Mahatma Gandhi (1869–1948)

Based on His attitude, ethics, teachings, and commandments; it is clear that Jesus could have nothing to do with the origins of Roman Catholicism. Jesus would not recognize or be associated with Roman Catholic structure, methods and evolution. If Jesus would appear today, the Roman Church would probably follow Isaiah 53, and treat Him like a leper. Based on its record, the Roman Church would probably try to quarantine and silence this Leper, and give Him the same kind of sentence their Roman predecessors gave Jesus almost two thousand years ago. The historical and real Jesus would most likely not be recognized or welcome in large portions of modern Christianity (37).

With respect to the hierarchical structure of the Roman Church, its riches, its property, its pomp and ritual and its many churches; Acts 17: 24-25 should be kept in mind: "God, who made the world and all that is in it, since He is Lord of heaven and earth, does not dwell in temples made by hands. Neither is He served with men's hands, as though He needed anything—." Many believe that the verses in Acts 17 indicate that "if you are looking for God in a church, you won't find Him there." In fact, the structure, imagery, riches, art, alleged holy articles and relics, worship tradition and statues within a Roman Church are rejected in Acts 17: 29: "Therefore, since we are the offspring of God, we ought not to think that the Divine Nature is like gold or silver or stone, something shaped by art and man's devising."

Also, there are a number of weaknesses in the claim of one ruler, one papal authority, one unbroken line of popes starting from St. Peter. The Bible and the Catholic Encyclopedia both support the fact that the first acknowledged leader of Christ's followers was St. James, not St. Peter. Peter has a leadership position among the apostles and the Jewish followers of Jesus. But, as stated in the Catholic Encyclopedia, James is, without a doubt, the Bishop of Jerusalem and the first leader of Christ's religious community (Acts 12: 17, Acts 15: 13, Acts 21: 18, Galatians 1: 19 and Galatians 2: 9-12).

"There is a destiny that makes us brothers, none goes his way alone. All that we send into the lives of others, comes back into our own." Edwin Markham (1852–1940)

Since St. Paul claimed that he has gospel teaching authority over the Gentiles and Peter has authority over the Jewish Christians (Galatians 2: 7), this eliminates the possibility that St. Peter could be considered the head (or original pope) for the Pauline dominated Christianity of today. If Jesus ever did declare Peter "the rock" upon which he would build His church, and given Peter any "keys," His declaration to Peter would have been associated with the structure of the original Jerusalem community. Setting aside the questionable claims made by St. Paul, Jesus was not involved with a Pauline Gentile church that was initiated and formed 20 to 30 years after his crucifixion. And Jesus was certainly not a willing participant in the formation of the Roman Catholic Church Christian/Pagan hybrid, which appeared over 270 years later.

As Christianity was in its formative stages, there were quite a few Christian churches; with Antioch, Alexandria, Rome, Constantinople and Jerusalem being the dominant church centers from the first through the fourth centuries. The bishops of these church centers were referred to as patriarchs, and the Patriarchs of Rome, Alexandria and Antioch appear in the oldest versions of canon law.

Rome was considered "special" by Iranaeus, Bishop of Lyon (125–202 A.D.), and Ignatius of Antioch (50–117 A.D.), due to its political, cultural and economic influence (3). However, the centers of Christian learning were in Antioch and Alexandria. There is no credible reference to any Roman papal authority having ultimate control over the rest of Christian churches at that time (23). From 252 to 380 A.D., with more than ten church councils being held in Antioch, the Patriarch of Antioch had precedence over the Patriarchs of Alexandria, Rome, Constantinople and Jerusalem. The use of the term pope to indicate a higher level of power and oversight appears to have been initiated, later on, by the Patriarchs of Alexandria and Rome.

"By persuasion, not by violence, are men to be won to the Faith." St. Bernard of Clairvaux (1090–1153)

In Rome, papal power and authority appears to have evolved during the fifth and sixth centuries, taking hundreds of years to become what it is today. Many centuries passed before a pope could speak as the head of the church. Prior to that time, all major decisions affecting the Christian churches had to be settled by all patriarchs and bishops meeting together in council. The Bishops of Rome, Damasus I (366–383 A.D.) and Zosimus (417–418 A.D.) tried, unsuccessfully to establish authority and influence over the African churches in settling disputes. Bishops, patriarchs and other leaders rejected the Roman Church's attempts to establish this kind of supremacy or precedence (23, 38).

Apparently, Siricius (384–399 A.D.) was the first Bishop of Rome to be referred to as "pope." Pope Leo I (440–461 A.D.) was the first to claim that the Bishop of Rome was the preeminent and highest ranking Bishop of the Roman Catholic Church (23). However, Galatians 3: 25-26 says that "The Law has been our tutor unto Christ, that we might be justified by faith. But now that faith has come, we are no longer under a tutor. For you are all children of God through faith in Christ Jesus." In Matthew 23: 8-10, Jesus is quite explicit about not calling anyone on earth our father, "And call no one on earth your father; for One is your Father Who is in heaven." In 1 Timothy 2:5 "for there is one God and one Mediator between God and men, the Man Christ Jesus." Apparently, if we decide to take Jesus seriously, once we acquire a genuine faith, we no longer need a tutor, an earthly overlord or pope.

The papacy has a history of being politicized, used to promote wholesale slaughter, sold, abandoned, duplicated and immersed in fraud. According to Fr. Hans Küng, the alleged hand-off to Linus as the second pope appears to be a second century fraud (3). But that does not even begin to tell the story. Taking the Roman papacy seriously is very difficult to do when one looks at history and analyzes the claims of: 1) alleged papal links to Jesus through St. Peter, 2) papal authority, 3) papal debauchery and 4) the basis of papal infallibility dogma.

> "To consign a heretic to death is to commit an offence beyond atonement. God forbids their execution." St. John Chrysostom (347–407 A.D.)

St. Peter did not insist that he had a special rank above the other apostles. And St. Paul was very vocal about making sure that Peter and other members of the faith community were aware of that fact. St. Paul tempered his tendency to ignore James and scold Peter by occasionally acknowledging their leadership of the Jewish followers of Christ. But, there is no statement from Peter where he claims to be anything special. In Acts 10: 25-26, Peter says to Cornelius, "Stand up, I myself also am a man." Peter never claims to be "the Rock" and he does not claim to have supreme power and authority over the followers of Jesus.

During the first two hundred years of Christianity, there was no papal head. There were five Patriarchs of the Christian Church; and the Bishop of Rome was just one of them. At times, the Patriarchs of Alexandria, Antioch, Constantinople and Jerusalem had to reject, scold and lecture the Patriarch of Rome. Rome was often the "problem child" of the group as it attempted to intervene or dictate in certain religious or political matters (3, 23, 38). Eventually, Rome did succeed in its efforts to be preeminent. However, the papacy did not start on the path to become the office and base of power that exists today, until the fourth and fifth centuries.

Out of 271 people designated as "pope" by the Roman Catholic Church, 64 met with violent deaths, many from being poisoned by fellow clergy. Leo III and John XVI were mutilated. Up until Zephyrinus made up his mind about the divinity of Christ, some of the so-called popes prior to Zephyrinus did not believe in this doctrine. Excluding the Avignon popes who were deposed, exiled or expelled; 28 popes sold the so called "Chair of St. Peter" to foreigners. The papacy was essentially the property of various families including the house of Theophylact and the Medici family, for more than 150 years (23, 39). Some cardinals and popes were appointed in their early teens.

"However, it is a fundamental human right, a privilege of nature, that every man should worship according to his own convictions: one man's religion nether harms nor helps another man. It is assured by no part of religion to compel religion." Tertullian (160–220 A.D.)

Many clergy insist that there were not many bad popes, maybe ten at the most. The Catholic Encyclopedia goes into detail on just a few bad popes, such as Rodrigo Borgia (Pope Alexander VI) who was the model for Machiavelli. In truth, the number of horribly corrupt and savagely cruel popes boggles the mind.

Some popes listed in the Catholic Encyclopedia were condemned, and some were condemned for heresy. Marcellinus (296–304 A.D.), a canonized saint, allegedly practiced pagan ritual. Damasus I, another canonized saint (but often referred to as "the matron's ear tickler") was brought to trial for adultery. He was rescued at the last minute by the Emperor, Gratian. St. Jerome warned that the Church of Rome, under Damasus I, was monstrously corrupt. Eusebius was Constantine's propaganda minister, and some of his propaganda defied even the wildest of imaginations. Pope Honorius I (625–638 A.D.) was condemned as a heretic, and this condemnation was confirmed by Pope Leo II.

Considering a few of the, allegedly, more corrupt popes: Clement V, Benedict IX, Clement VI, Clement VII, John XI, Alexander VI, John XII, Sixtus IV, John XIII, Innocent III, John XV, Sergius III, Pius II, Leo VIII, Julius II, Paul III, Julius III, Innocent VII, Leo X and Innocent VIII; we have murder, mass murder, adultery, pedophilia, indolence, extravagance, avarice, incest, simony, the establishment of a Lateran brothel and, according to a number of clergy and church doctors, some of the cruelest and evil men to walk the face of this earth (3, 23, 38, 39). Pope Leo I (440–461 A.D.), a canonized saint who confronted Attila the Hun, has been described by some as a sadistic torturer. Sergius III (904–911) murdered his predecessor and predecessor's rival. His affair with the 15 year old Marozia produced a son who later became the debauched Pope John XI (931–935). A few years later, Pope John XII (955–963) became pontiff at age 16. Apparently, he was not the youngest pope in this so-called direct line to St. Peter.

"It is a damned and bloody work, the graceless action of a heavy hand."
William Shakespeare (1564–1616), from King John IV

Benedict V (964) was stripped of his vestments in 964. The claim that he was pontiff for any appreciable length of time is highly questionable. Pope John XII (955–963) was described as a sadistic adulterer, defiling his father's concubine and his own niece. He may have been killed by his lover's husband. Pope John XIII (965–972) was apparently no better. Antipope Boniface VII (974, 984–85) was described as a horrid monster by Pope Sylvester II (999–1003).

But the insult to God's integrity and intelligence continues. The doctrine of papal infallibility forces the Holy Spirit to interact with, support, advise, and approve the actions of many papal miscreants who are some of the most corrupt, debauched, cruel and irreverent leaders of history. Some refer to the doctrine of infallibility as a true sin against the Holy Spirit. Pope John XXII (a despot in his own right), in his papal Bull *Qui quorundum* (1324), referred to beliefs or doctrines of papal infallibility as "the work of the devil." Driven by his own political motives, John XXII cancelled all previous papal infallibility claims.

If the specifications for deacons and bishops described in 1 Timothy 3: 1-14 are to be taken seriously, of the 271 so-called "popes," at least 100 of them fail to meet the minimum standards required for their position. In 1 Timothy 1-13, a bishop must be "blameless, the husband of one wife, temperate, sober-minded, of good behavior, hospitable, able to teach, not given to wine, not greedy for money, gentle, not quarrelsome, not covetous, able to rule his own house, not a novice, not puffed up with pride, have a good testimony from others, be above reproach, reverent and pure of conscience." The failure of many popes and many Roman Catholic clergy to meet the minimum requirements for their office, as stated in 1 Timothy, is further evidence of a lack of papal continuity and credibility. Obviously, there are huge gaps and discrepancies in any claim of a direct papal line to Jesus of Nazareth, through St. Peter.

> *"But we have forgotten God. We have forgotten the gracious hand, which preserved us in peace and multiplied and enriched and strengthened us. And we have vainly imagined, in the deceitfulness of our hearts, that all these blessings were produced by some superior virtue and wisdom of our own."*
> Abraham Lincoln (1809–1865)

Some will argue, that the Roman Church has survived this long in spite of its depravity and corruption, and this proves that the Holy Spirit is at work keeping the Roman Catholic Church doctrinally pure. In truth, the reason that the Roman Church has survived so long is that it was a unifying state religion that helped to prop up and stabilize a decaying Roman Empire, and it became one of the last remnants of that empire. Then, just before it was about to collapse, the Roman Catholic Church found a new mission, and prospered, because it served as a very low cost vehicle to colonize the Americas.

Is the papal line unbroken and infallible? Many clerics, from Bishop Joseph G. Strossmayer to Fr. Hans Küng (3, 23) have clearly shown, the conclusion would have to be "No!" on both counts. The evidence indicates that some of the popes were heretics, murderers and sexual deviants—they were essentially anti-Christ. To make matters worse, many of popes could not even come close to meeting the basic qualifications for a bishop or deacon as specified in 1 Timothy. The papacy was owned by several families and bought and sold many times. These facts nullify any claim of a legitimate papal linkage to Jesus and St. Peter, and any claim for infallibility.

All one has to do is ask, "Would Jesus approve what has been done by the Roman Church, in His Name? Remember, in Matthew 16: 23, Jesus said to Peter, "You are an offense to me, for you are not mindful of the things of God, but of the things of men." In Matthew 18: 21-33, Jesus condemns unjust business practices. In Luke 17: 2, Mark 9: 41 and Matthew 18: 6; Jesus says, "But whoever causes one of these little ones, who believe in me to sin, it would be better for him if a millstone were hung around his neck, and he were drowned in the depth of the sea." In these Gospels, Jesus appears to be referring to children and those Christians who are new in their faith.

"Infallibility is a pestiferous doctrine, a pernicious audacity." Pope John XXII, in his 1324 papal bull

In Matthew 7: 15-23, Jesus condemns false prophets and criminal behavior (those who practice lawlessness). Jesus says that a good tree cannot bear bad fruit and a bad tree cannot bear good fruit and, "by their fruits, ye shall know them." The Word of Jesus strongly indicates that the bad fruit of the Roman Church (hiding pedophilia crimes committed by clergy and hierarchy, simony, debauchery, murder, corrupt financial practices, war crimes, criminal behavior, Crusades, Inquisition, etc.) is strong proof that the Roman Church became a "bad tree." Would the statement that Jesus made in Matthew 18: 6 indicate that Christianity would have been better off if a millstone had been hung around the neck of the Roman Church, and it were drowned in the depths of the sea?

Did Jesus give any hint that he would want to be associated with the initiation and evolution of a corporate Roman Church structure?" In John 3: 15-16, John 6: 35,37, Mark 12: 30-31 and Luke 17: 21; Jesus says, "No!" In John 2: 16 and Matthew 23: 1-33, Jesus says, "Hell No!" "You hypocrites, you blind guides, fools, you serpents and brood of vipers! You, who are full of extortion and self-indulgence. How can you escape condemnation?" Some of the attitudes and actions of the Roman Catholic Church would probably be as insulting, repulsive and horrifying to Jesus in the same way as primitive slaughter, genocide and deal making and appeasement through ritual child sacrifice would be to His sensitivities.

Jesus did not "hint" about his likes and dislikes. He appears to have given a very clear negative answer to any question concerning the validity of the papacy, Roman Church hierarchy and Roman Church methods—many times, and in many ways. To claim that the Roman Church represents the interests and teachings of Jesus adds more insult to a 1,700 year old blasphemy.

"The Catholic Church, headquartered in Rome, succumbed to the reforms of the Roman Emperors. It was a religion Jesus would have deplored." William Bramley, from his book, *The Gods of Eden* (1993)

9. CATHOLIC CANON LAW: DOES IT HAVE A VALID FOUNDATION?

A canon is often defined as a rule, model, standard, regulation or dogma decreed by a church council. Early Christian communities were guided by customs and traditions, handed down from generation to generation. These communities were not particularly legalistic. But, they did have community rules and Scripture driven rules (some very strict). In his letters to certain communities, St. Paul was quite clear on the proper place for "the law." "Knowing that a man is not justified by the works of the law but by faith in Jesus Christ—for by the works of the law no flesh shall be justified—for I through the law have died to the law that I might live to God." (Galatians 2: 19) "If you are led by the spirit, you are not under the law." (Galatians 5: 18) "For all of the law is fulfilled in one word, even in this: You shall love your neighbor as yourself." (Galatians 5: 14) "For Christ is the consummation of the law unto justice for everyone who believes." (Romans 10: 4)

To the early Christian communities, Paul's letters provided all the legal structure they needed. It was simple; the only law they needed involved those teachings and customs handed down by Jesus of Nazareth. The teachings of Jesus had priority over secular law. This attitude had serious effects on these Christian communities, costing many Christians their lives and lives of their families.

As the Roman Catholic state religion evolved, the Church began to see itself as an authoritative entity that had the power and political influence to make its own rules and impose legal constraints. In 314 A.D., Under the reign of Constantine, twenty five canons were issued that dealt mostly with internal church problems. Eleven years later, these canons were applied to the Christian church faithful.

"The first thing we do, let's kill all the lawyers." William Shakespeare (1564–1616), from Henry VI, part 2

The problem with Roman Church canon law is that, in some areas, it appears to have the same kind of devious background and malicious intent that was characteristic of German law under the influence of the Nazi regime in the 1930's and 1940's. Also, in certain aspects of Roman Church canon law, application and enforcement appears to be directly or indirectly based on forged documents (40). These include the Donation of Constantine (alleged donation of vast territories in Western Roman Empire to the Roman Church, by the Emperor Constantine), the Pseudo-Isidorian Forgeries (protection of clerical property, judicial authority of the bishops, bishops immune from prosecution in secular courts, justification of papal power and authority, papal link to St. Peter) and the Symmachian Forgeries (claimed that the pope could be judged by no human authority).

The requirement for a group of canons to establish norms for early church organization, structure and ecclesiastical discipline is certainly understandable. Some of the original 20 canons of the Council of Nicea (325 A.D.) were instituted to incorporate rules on the appointment of bishops and to establish the primacy of the Churches of Alexandria, Antioch and Rome (40). In some of these canons, clergy could not practice usury, certain clergy were not permitted to live with women unless they were related, rapid promotion of converts to hierarchical positions was not allowed, the relationship between the various member churches was defined and eunuchs were excluded from the clergy.

But, by the ninth century, canon law was becoming perverse and highly self-serving within the Roman Church. The Pseudo-Isadorian Forgeries were used as the basis of credibility to argue that the Bishop of Rome had absolute primacy since apostolic times. That primacy claim still remains today.

"The degree of Doctor of Canon Law (JCD) is one of the most unusual examples of academic game-playing still to survive in our society. No theology should support such nonsense. Canon law has little to do with education, and practically nothing to do with creative and theological thought."
Fr. James Kavanaugh, from his book, *A Modern Priest Looks at His Outdated Church* (1968)

The Pseudo-Isadorian Forgeries were used to "prove" that papal authority was universal and that certain political systems favorable to the Roman Church had legitimacy. Even after the Roman Catholic Church realized that these documents were nothing more than massive forgeries, these fraudulent documents continue to influence and validate Roman Church dogma up to and including the dogma of papal infallibility.

Canon law is still heavily influenced by the knowledge base and political/economic control systems of the 12th and 13th centuries (41). As time went on and as the dictatorship of the Roman Church grew, canon law became an instrument to legalize immoral and heinous acts, similar to what was done in Nazi Germany prior to WW II. Excommunication doctrines and "just punishment" were established for heretics and various troublesome sects. The acquisition of property from victims of Roman Church justice was validated and justified by various canons.

A wide range of crimes committed against humanity during the Crusades and the Inquisition were "justified" by canon law (including some very brutal papal judicial, legislative, "just war" and enforcement doctrines). Whenever a new justification was needed; like magic, an appropriate papal decretal or council decretal would appear.

The lack of moral responsibility and responsibility by the U.S. Bishops in their attempts to conceal or destroy evidence and transfer pedophile priests has a strong link to hierarchical privilege provided by canon law.

Canon 1341 instructs bishops to first apply "fraternal correction or reproof" and "methods of pastoral care" with wrongdoers in the clergy. These wrongdoers include priests who have been repeatedly guilty of sexual crimes including pedophilia and ephebophilia. According to canon law and church policies, the clergy violator is counseled, isolated, protected, transferred and forgiven for committing multiple heinous and unspeakable crimes against "the little ones."

> *"The mistreatment of children (by the Roman Catholic Church) was so massive and so prolonged, that it borders on the unbelievable."* July 23, 2003 Report from the Massachusetts Attorney General Thomas F. Reilly

Canon 1395: 2 states that sex between priests and minors is an ecclesiastical crime. However, the code commentary states that an initial charge of molestation of a minor is "not viewed as seriously" as cohabiting with a woman or attempted marriage! A priest who marries a woman is often suspended or excommunicated and never forgiven; while the priest who commits acts the egregious act of pedophilia receives council, protection and forgiveness.

In his analysis of fraudulent claims made by the Roman Catholic Church, Fr. Hans Küng makes the point that the forgeries that served as the basis for canon law and papal power are "so pernicious" because "they have an effect on the way in which the church understands itself (23)." Fr. Küng points out that the legitimacy of the papacy and the doctrine of infallibility are based on a number of canons that are derived from known forged decretals, including the Pseudo-Isidorian decretal canon laws that were written in the ninth century. And he states, "the control of Rome over the whole Catholic Church, over local, regional and national churches, over bishops, clergy and individual believers, indeed even over the ecumenical councils, was given a legal basis unscrupulously by means of these forged decretals (3, 23)."

A number of attorneys, who have the task to litigate against a highly "compromised" Roman Catholic Church, "that is immersed in denial," are sickened by the actions and attitude of the Church hierarchy. One Roman Catholic lawyer stated that, when taking depositions from bishops and chancellors, the documented truth is staring right at you, "and they look at you and deny! Denial is at the core of the problem. It radically reforms your view of the hierarchy." After their experiences with the attitude and methods of an errant and despotic Roman Catholic Church, some of these attorneys will no longer send their children to Catholic schools, and they will not let their children be altar servers (42).

"Jesus wept." John 11: 35

We can stop right here, and ask ourselves several questions. "Does Roman Catholic canon law have any basis of credibility? Does canon law have a valid foundation?" The evidence shows that these legal canonic entities contain a massive amount of forgery, perverse intent and last minute "adaptation." Every time the Roman Church wanted to establish or enhance its base of power, every time the Roman Church wanted to acquire more territory and property, every time the Roman Church wanted to destroy a troublesome belief system; the appropriate legal documents would suddenly appear, and the Church had its way.

After reading the history of canon law, the conclusions concerning the necessity of retraction or reform, reached by Fr. James Kavanaugh and Fr. Hans Küng, appear to be valid, and understated. The genetic make-up associated with the structure and body of Roman Church canon law contains huge numbers of components that are immersed in fraud, forgery, theft and obvious game playing. The kind of game playing that is done in canon law was rejected by Jesus, in Matthew 23 and Paul in Galatians 2 and 5, and Romans 10.

The claim is often made that Isaiah 54 is the prophecy for the coming of the Roman Catholic Church. But the content of Isaiah 54: 14 eliminates any possibility that this claim could be legitimate; "And <u>thou shall be</u> <u>founded in justice</u>: <u>depart far from oppression,</u> <u>for thou shalt not fear;</u> <u>and from terror, for it shall not come near thee</u>." Isaiah 54: 14 is the antithesis of the Roman Church. The Roman Church was founded on terror, oppression and fear. It developed and used a highly unjust, fraud based and self-serving system of canon law. Isaiah 54: 17 appears to provide protection for the "bulwarks and gates" of Christianity, indicating that any unjust and oppressive corporate religious structure is ultimately doomed to failure, and will be condemned.

Canon law is more of "satan's smoke." The basis and structure of canon law can not be taken seriously by Christians who believe in the highly non-legalistic, simple, loving and all inclusive teachings of Jesus.

"Ninety nine percent of lawyers give the rest a bad name." Steven Wright

10. CAN THE ROMAN CATHOLIC CHURCH SAVE ITS OWN SOUL?

With continued revelations of sex-abuse scandals, cover-ups, financial scandals and a wide variety of associated criminal activities in the Roman Catholic Church; the front cover of the April 1, 2002 issue of U.S. News and World Report asked the question; "Can the Church save its soul?" The article, "*Catholics in Crisis*," provided some interesting background and insight. It stated, "There were new signs of recognition at the church's highest levels that the scandal could no longer be dismissed as the regrettable, but controllable, perversions of a few priests. Rather, it is a full blown cancer, threatening to sap the church of its moral authority, public trust and financial resources." A statement from Pope John Paul II was also revealing; "As priests, we are personally and profoundly affected by the sins of some of our brothers who have betrayed the grace of ordination." The words "sins of some of our brothers" reveal the tremendous state of self deception and denial that is characteristic of Roman Catholic hierarchy.

An investigation by the Dallas Morning News, published in June of 2002, revealed that two thirds of US bishops participated in protecting, hiding or transferring priests who were guilty of various sex crimes. Many bishops around the world (in Great Britain, France, Austria, Poland, Australia, Canada, Mexico, Ireland, Italy, South America, etc.) appear to be guilty of these same criminal acts. The Vatican has been a repository of incriminating documentation revealing the criminal activities, perversity and sex crimes of many errant priests and hierarchy. The group of betrayers designated by the pope as "some of our brothers" includes more than 4% of U.S. priests, that served during the study time (24), and 67% of the US bishops.

> "For the Church in the Western world, the recent sexual abuse scandal is probably the biggest crisis we've yet faced, though it's not so much a crisis of faith as one of credibility. It is not the press that's causing this scandal. God's hand is behind this, humbling and purifying us. The real issue is not inflated anti-clerical press coverage, but our infidelity, and God's pruning hand. If the price tag is humiliation and a drain on our resources, so be it." Rev. Ron Rolheiser, OMI

In the June 2003 issue of the National Catholic Reporter, the article "Bread Rising" published the vow that every cardinal allegedly makes to the pope, "Never to reveal to anyone whatever has been confided to me in secret and the revelation of which could cause damage or dishonor to Holy Church." Obviously, if a vow like this is necessary, the Church is not "Holy," and not following the example of Jesus.

This vow promotes malfeasance and criminal behavior. This vow promotes deception and obstruction of justice. It is a vow that nourished more than 50 years of sexual misconduct with minors in the Boston Archdiocese, and centuries of misconduct in Europe and the Americas. The Roman Catholic Church's institutional acceptance of clergy sexual abuse of children (National Catholic Reporter, August 1, 2003, pg. 11) was "unbelievable" according to Massachusetts Attorney General, Thomas Reilly. In a letter to Bishop Wilton Gregory, former Oklahoma Governor Frank Keating stated that with respect to the Catholic hierarchy's practice of "secrecy, resisting subpoenas" and tendency to "deny, obfuscate and explain away;" the Roman Church's actions are the "model of a criminal organization."

There are consequences that must be faced and a price that must be paid for the arrogant, closed and secretive structure of a church, that has been entirely unaccountable to the community and legal authorities. As stated in the May 31 issue of the National Catholic Reporter (pg. 7, Letters to the Editor), "The real causes of for the depth of the present crisis are an improper use of authority and the pathology of secrecy, silence and deceit that begin in the highest offices of the church and filters down." In Luke 12: 2-3, Jesus says, "Everything that is hidden will be found out, and every secret will be known. Whatever you say in the dark will be heard when it is day. Whatever you whisper in a closed room will be shouted from the housetops." In essence, Jesus is saying that "consequences must be faced and a price will be paid" for this kind of institutional arrogance and corruption.

"Every day, people are straying away from the church and going back to God." Lenny Bruce (1925–1966)

It is now clear that many bishops all over the world have been guilty of either directly or indirectly participating in these kinds of criminal activities, including the Vatican itself! The words, "sins of some of our brothers" provides the basis for a vast understatement. A more truthful statement from the pope would have been, "sins committed by many of the Church's hierarchy, and by many of our brother priests." The pope cannot claim ignorance or innocence, and he cannot be excluded from this group of nefarious characters and miscreants. A title appears near the end of the National Catholic Reporter article, which may provide an accurate characterization of the Roman Church as being "Not just morally bankrupt"—but maybe worse.

The National Catholic Reporter article goes on to give some hope to those who want to see the Roman Catholic Church change, but survive. It has been stated many times that corruption starts at the top, and reform starts at the bottom of any church organization. Many Catholic faithful feel that if the laity have more control, that can help to help to make Roman Church trustworthy and morally responsible.

But the question has to be asked; "Was the Roman Church ever trustworthy and morally responsible?" At any time since its inception, would Jesus of Nazareth give the Roman Church anything above an F or D grade in areas such as 1) following the teachings of Jesus, 2) following the example of Jesus, 3) being trustworthy, 4) following high moral standards consistently, 5) being just and merciful or 6) being tolerant?

It is doubtful that the Roman Catholic Church could have ever received passing grades from Jesus. In its sordid history, the Roman Church has embraced very few characteristics that reflect the teachings of Jesus. This is not surprising considering the brutal methods and reputation of a decadent Roman Empire that served, and still serves, as the basic foundation of the Roman Catholic Church.

"We are always making God our accomplice, that so we may legalize our own inequities." Henri Frederic Amiel (1821–1881)

As stated in the May 31, 2002 issue of the National Catholic Reporter (pg. 24, Letters to the Editor), early Christians, right up to St. John Chrysostom and Pelagius, believed in the freedom of religious choice and the responsibility of the individual. Religion was not to be forced on anyone. However, under the restrictive and brutal Roman influence combined with St. Augustine's belief that mankind and nature were essentially evil, the authority of the church took over. The excuse used was that harsh measures were necessary in order to maintain control over the influence of the officially designated evils. The supreme virtue that promoted "good" was obedience. With this attitude, it did not take long for a variety of corrupt, murderous and brutal practices or activities to become quite acceptable; including burning at the stake, acquisition of victim's property, endless torture, the Crusades, the Inquisition, etc. The papacy grew in power. By the time Gregory the Great became pope, as Lord Acton indicated, the papacy became a major participant in the "absolute power that corrupts."

The Roman Church is the last remnant of a decaying and brutal empire. The Roman Catholic Church reflects its origins, attitudes and characteristics of the Roman Empire. And much of what the Roman Empire represented was loathsome to Jesus.

As far as some Catholics are concerned, the Roman Catholic Church cannot save its own soul until it completes one very basic, but terribly difficult, task. It must remove the word "Roman" from its name. It must remove any trace of Vatican rule from its governing structure. It must become the more Christ-inspired group that it was, prior to its takeover by the Roman Empire. It must become more of what Jesus was and what Jesus taught. It must acquire the "essence" of Christianity and become a belief system that reflects the teachings of Jesus (18, 23, 37). It must become something that can instill pride in all of us rather than shock, embarrassment, shame or loathing.

"Man is kind enough when he is not excited by religion." Mark Twain (1835–1910)

Paintings and statues of the Trinity are on display in the Vatican. But They, (God, Jesus, Holy Spirit) are not present in the Vatican, and never were. Some Catholic clergy have provided an interesting description of the power that appears to be in control of the Vatican—and the power that controls is definitely not God the Father, God the Son or God the Holy Spirit. As far as some Catholic clergy are concerned, it is another much more troublesome character that occupies and influences the entire length, breadth and depth of the Vatican.

Catholics might wonder, "What is the future of the Roman Catholic Church, if it makes no attempt to save its own soul?" We don't have to look very far for answers. In his book, *Uses of the Past*, Herbert Muller mentions the crude forgeries, produced during the time of Charlemagne, that made up the Donation of Constantine and the False Decretals of Isadore (4). These forgeries were unquestioned by medieval scholars who were not bold enough to expose them. This lack of scrutiny served the purposes of the Roman Church for more than 800 years, providing the soft, false, unstable and unsubstantiated foundations for papal power and the dogma of infallibility. What Muller describes is a chilling reminder of what is written in Daniel 2: 1-33. Daniel reveals the meaning of King Nebuchadnezzor's dreams. One of the dreams involves "a great statue—tall of stature—and the look thereof was terrible." The head of this statue was "of fine gold, the breast and arms of silver, the belly and thighs of brass, the legs of iron and the feet part of iron and part of clay."

Under the right conditions, iron and clay can be very hard. When conditions change, iron and clay can both become very brittle and crumble. In verses 34–35, the destruction of the terrible statue was initiated when "a stone, cut out of a mountain, strikes the feet of iron and clay, breaking the statue to pieces." The pieces are, then, "carried away by the wind." The stone remains, becoming "a great mountain, filling the whole earth."

"Nothing great is easily won" Myron Medcalf's grandmother

The implications of Daniel's dream are devastating for a Roman Church that continues to defile the teachings of Jesus. Is Daniel 2: 31-35 a prophesy aimed directly at the self proclaimed custodians of Christianity, the Roman Catholic Church? Does the "head of fine gold and breast and arms of silver" represent the papacy and Church hierarchy? Does this also describe the wealth, the ill gotten gains, of the Church acquired by Crusades, Inquisitions, war crimes, persecutions and financial misdeeds? Is the "terrible look" associated with the abuse of power, conflict of interest, hypocrisy, brutality, sexual depravity and negligence that has been a well documented characteristic of Roman Church hierarchy?

In Revelation 17 and 18, is the harlot "sitting on the beast," "arrayed in purple and scarlet, adorned with precious stones and pearls," "drunk with blood of the saints and martyrs" who "sits on seven hills" a description of the hierarchical center of the Roman Church—the Vatican? For early Christians, the code word for Rome was Babylon. Does "Babylon the Great, the mother of harlots" refer to the center of papal power in Rome? And when the angel in Revelation 18 says, "Babylon the Great is fallen, and has become a dwelling place for demons, and a prison for every foul spirit," is this a prediction of the ultimate destruction of the last remnant of the Roman Empire, the Roman Catholic Church? From the 12th century's St. Malachy to this century's Fr. Hans Küng and Bishop Spong; many good Christians have predicted this kind of fate for the Roman Church. If Romans 1: 18 is to be taken seriously, God will not intervene as the Roman Church is destroyed; "For the Wrath of God is revealed from heaven against all ungodliness and unrighteousness of men, who suppress the truth in unrighteousness." Chapters 2 through 8, in this book, provide a massive amount of documented evidence concerning the unrighteousness and suppression of truth that has occurred for centuries in the Roman Catholic Church.

"Continue to contaminate your own bed and you will one night suffocate in your own waste." Chief Seattle, Suquamish (1786–1866)

If Catholicism is left in the hands of the Roman Catholic Church, current trends indicate that it will die a terrible death, and possibly pull down a significant amount of Christianity with it. No matter how much they want to deny it, all Christian religions and Christian belief systems have a strong genetic link to the Roman Church. It would be a crime and a shame to allow the beauty of Catholicism and the wide variety of valuable Christian beliefs to be disfigured and ultimately destroyed by the Roman influence. By returning to a more democratic family of highly related belief systems; where dialogue, debate and honest questions are welcome; a healthier, happier and more Christ-like religious climate could return. However, if Catholicism is to survive, the Roman influence must be removed—completely.

In Daniel 2, the legs of iron and the feet of iron and clay would appear to describe the political compromise, shaky foundation and dark side of a church with its origins linked to a corrupt and decaying Roman Empire. Like Daniel's statue "with a terrible look," the Roman Church appears to be on the verge of being struck down by its own arrogance and decadence and swept away by the winds of discovery, dissent and decency. If the foundation and fabric of the Roman Church are truly represented by the terrible statue in the Book of Daniel, then there is nothing on the face of this earth that can save the Roman Catholic Church from itself. The huge stone that will strike it down is the Ultimate Dissenter and the real Cornerstone of Christianity, Jesus of Nazareth.

In Matthew 16: 23, as the Ultimate Dissenter, Jesus appears to be rebuking, the entire Roman Church when He says, "Get behind me satan, thou art a scandal to me; for thou dost not mind not the things of God, but those of men."

"From some fissure, the smoke of satan entered into the sanctuary of the Church." Pope Paul VI (1897–1978), Allegedly, stated during the Ninth Anniversary of his coronation

11. HOW MIGHTY IS GOD ALMIGHTY?

In early times, most people thought of "God Almighty" as being the creator, ruler and caretaker of heaven (a place in the clouds about 5 miles to 100 miles above their heads) and the earth disk floating on an infinite ocean. For them, the earth was a region below the "firmament," several thousands of miles in diameter (43). It was easy to imagine a Yaweh, Jehovah, God, Allah, Great Spirit, etc. who watched over and actively participated in the events associated with tribal people in a relatively small land mass.

As explorers circled the globe, religious leaders began to realize that the estimates of the earth's shape and size, made by the Greek Eratosthenese (third century B.C.), were correct. The earth was spherical, and the earth was bigger than they first thought. The estimates for the earth's diameter made by Eratosthenese were close to 8,000 miles. The previous numbers were corrected, based on new knowledge. Now, God's updated domain was a more substantive earth-firmament region involving a centrally located sphere, with point-to-point distances, ranging from approximately 8,000 miles in diameter ($8 \cdot 10^3$ miles) to 25,000 miles in circumference ($25 \cdot 10^3$ miles). This earthly entity, along with the heavens and the waters, was what God created and what He ruled. But that dogma had a short lifetime. As science progressed, the earth, the firmament and God's creation became more complicated and much larger. As the church resisted the introduction of new knowledge, and even while the Inquisition silenced or murdered those who provided this new knowledge, church leaders had to recognize the fact that the earth did not occupy the high and mighty place they once thought. The earth was no longer the center of the universe. The earth was just "one of many." God's creation involved large heavenly bodies and great distances.

> "There is a theory which states that if ever anybody discovers exactly what the Universe is for and why it is here, it will instantly disappear and be replaced by something even more bizarre and inexplicable. There is another theory that states this has already happened." Douglas Adams (1952–2001)

All of a sudden, the tribal concept of a God who participates in killing off undesirables, changes his mind, screws up and rules like a local dictator; was beginning to look ridiculous. God had a lot more to look after than religious leaders initially realized.

Science was relentless, and new knowledge continued to pour in. Church leaders had to face the fact that they were dealing with a God Who was much bigger than they had originally thought. A solar system that has a radius of more than 3,000,000,000 miles ($3 \cdot 10^9$ miles, or 3 billion miles) was a painful enough reality for a church hierarchy to face. But then, they were really knocked off balance when informed that we are living in a very large galaxy that may be more than 600,000,000,000,000,000 miles ($6 \cdot 10^{17}$ miles) wide; containing billions of stars, many of which are like our sun (6, 44).

But it doesn't stop there. More powerful telescopes (both radio and optical) and computer models indicate that our universe is filamentary—like the cytoskeleton of a living cell (45), self replicating (46), self regulating (homeostasis) and connected to other universes in a volume that may involve four or more spatial dimensions (47). Our universe appears to be much like a living cell that is connected to other living cells, forming a larger and more complicated living structure. And current estimates for the size of our universe indicate it has a radius that is in excess of the Hubble distance of approximately 83,000,000,000,000,000,000,000 miles ($8.3 \cdot 10^{22}$ miles), and is expanding in size by more than 20% every billion years.

It takes about 4.2 to 4.3 years for photons of light from the nearest stars (Proxima Centauri and Alpha Centauri A & B) to reach the earth. Light from the closest galaxy to us, M 31 or the Great Andromeda Galaxy, requires about two million years ($2 \cdot 10^6$ years) to reach us. At 186,000 miles per second, a beam of light requires more than 14 billion years (more than $14 \cdot 10^9$ years) to travel across our universe. The awesome Creator of all this must be incredibly and extremely "Mighty."

"Photons have mass?!? I didn't even know they were Catholic." Woody Allen

With approximately 100 billion galaxies in the universe, and each galaxy containing 100 billion stars; if only one intelligent life form were allowed per galaxy, that would amount to more than 100 billion (10^{11}) planets with life forms similar (or not so similar) to our own. It would appear that God has a lot of creatures to look after. Like Santa, does God need a lot of little helpers to look after 100,000,000,000 life supporting planets, and possibly 600,000,000,000,000,000,000 intelligent beings with souls, prayers, hopes and fears in just one universe?

The astronomer, Fred Hoyle, claimed there is evidence that matter (primarily hydrogen) is being created continuously (44). He stated, "Many atoms that are in existence today did not exist in the past and many of the atoms in the universe that will be in existence in the future do not exist today." Some estimates indicate that hydrogen is being continuously created in our universe at a rate of 10^{32} tons per second. If this is true, What, or Who, is creating all of this additional matter? Structuring and managing a 100 million light year universe, requiring the continuous creation of approximately 10^{32} tons per second of hydrogen and something in excess of 600,000,000,000,000,000,000 different kinds of living souls would be stressful enough for any god, but it appears that there are more universes, just like ours, to oversee.

The universe may be something similar to what is described in John White's book, *Pole Shift* (48). Using variants of the anthropic principle and theories of time-varying cosmological constants (49, 50), our universe and the neighboring universes may be evolving living cells, and components of a larger living system. For the most part, like the living systems that we can analyze with a microscope or a physical exam, our universe could be benevolent and self-regulating with a tendency to seek a reasonably low energy state and an ability to preserve order. Native Americans have been trying to tell us for years that the universe is interconnected and alive—and all things have life.

> "Astronomy leads us to a unique event, a universe which was created out of nothing, one with the very delicate balance needed to provide exactly the conditions required to permit life, and one which has an underlying (one might say 'supernatural') plan." Arno Penzias

Many scientists see the universe as a violent place. This view would appear to be a very limited from the standpoint of the way our Creator has positioned us. A nice warm fire in a fireplace can provide significant warmth and comfort. However, the same fireplace fire, that gives us warmth and comfort, can be considered extremely violent if we are actually sitting in the middle of the fire. In a similar way, the universe, and its galaxies, have regions of high energy in order to keep living things "warm and cozy" at the outer fringes. We are not far from the outer rim of our own galaxy. That keeps us safe and keeps us far enough away from the "inner fires" to avoid being burned by exploding stars and ripped apart by black holes. There is ample evidence that the hand of God protects us. We have a sun that is not too close, and not too far, giving us warmth, energy and life. We have a moon that is just close enough to prevent each ocean wave from becoming a tsunami. We also have some very large outer planets that sweep through our solar system providing protection for us from a barrage of incoming Oort cloud and Kuiper belt debris. Without these four large outer planets, we would have a lot more to worry about than just an occasional asteroid impact.

It is very apparent that God has been severely underestimated and trivialized in our sacred writings. In those same writings, God has also been severely maligned and slandered. God Almighty is much more "Mighty," much more thoughtful, much more protective and much more benevolent than we ever imagined.

We are blessed and protected. We have been given a very precious gift, the joy of life. But that gift is a privilege, not a right. And if the universe is a living entity with a survival instinct, it will attempt to destroy us when we become malignant. This is not the Wrath of God. It is merely the consequence, that we bring on ourselves. This is a natural and pre-programmed outcome that will occur if we become malignant, hostile and dangerous in a benevolent environment that exists to serve the best interests for all of its occupants.

"The exquisite order displayed by our scientific understanding of the physical world calls for the divine." Vera Kistiakowsky

Our own bodies and many species of plant life put up a good fight against malignant entities. A self-regulating universe will do the same. Anything corrupt, destructive or malignant will attract corrective action by a system that has an instinct for order and survival. And, I don't have to convince many people that one of the most destructive and malignant forces in our environment, and our lives, involves the brutality and intolerance of organized religion.

In 1983, the Infrared Astronomical Satellite (IRAS), detected heat from something that was thought to be about 50 billion miles away in the constellation Orion. The heat detected apparently "comes and goes." NASA's Space Infrared Telescope Facility (SIRTF) may be able to provide improved capabilities to detect whatever it is that is out there (51), and possibly heading our way. Some astronomers have speculated that the object might be the Sun's binary dark star companion (U.S. News and World Report, September 10, 1984, p. 74). Others believe it is something much larger, that is much further away. E.R. Harrison, an astronomer at the University of Massachusetts, reported in Nature (November 24, 1977) that the Sun has a characteristic "wobble" that could be the result of the Sun being bound to a binary companion (48). Many dispute this theory. However, looking at the planets and various moons, evidence of the effects of a large massive object, careening through the volume occupied by the Solar System, are everywhere. Our disheveled Solar System looks like it had a number of encounters with a "giant bowling ball."

For instance, Venus apparently has no significant magnetic field, and it rotates very slowly in retrograde (clockwise) motion (Earth rotates counter-clockwise). One day on Venus is very long, amounting to 243 Earth days. The axis of Uranus is tipped over, approximately 98 degrees. The poles of Uranus can face the Sun. Four of Jupiter's moons, one of Saturn's moons and one of Neptune's moons (Triton) orbit their respective planets in retrograde motion (backwards).

> *"What happens if a big asteroid hits Earth? Judging from realistic simulations involving a sledge hammer and a common laboratory frog, we can assume it will be pretty bad."* Dave Barry

These and other anomalies indicate that, in the past, something very large, traveling very fast, may have periodically interacted with the Solar System. If this event involved the Sun's binary companion, the Sun's companion will return. The spotty infrared data that we are now detecting may be the first hint of the dark star that is coming our way. If ancient writings, including Sumerian, Hebrew, Chinese, Mayan, Egyptian, Greek (Herodotus and Plato), Roman (Seneca) and Arab (Averrhoes), are to be taken seriously, there is a significant amount of evidence that the Earth has experienced near misses with very large entities, and has been turned on its axis a number of times (48, 52). Many of these theories have been ignored or highly criticized. But, one might wonder, "What are the motivating factors behind current attempts to detect infrared emissions for some very large and relatively dark objects in certain constellations?"

If we recognize that nature and the universe are self-regulating and order seeking, and if we have an appreciation for history; patterns of defeat and destruction are revealed for many structures and belief systems that have been malignant, destructive or disorderly. There are many examples: the Roman Empire, Napoleon's reign, Nazi Germany and Stalinist Communism to name a few. It would appear that many components of the Roman Catholic Church, Judaism, Protestantism, Mormonism and Islam also fall into this category. Historical records have shown that malignancies, corruption and destructive entities tend to attract destructive forces on both a small scale, and on a large scale. And if the intolerance and self-centered posture of organized religions become malignant and corrupt enough, they may attract a bigger and more massively destructive entity. That big Son-of-a-Bitch (BSB) that could be heading our way, approximately 50 billion miles out, might be attracted toward us more and more as we threaten the order and dignity of the universe with our religion, our politics, our sloppy ways and our self-interests. This could be nature's way of getting rid of the problem we are, and the problems we often create.

"These, Gentlemen are the opinions upon which I base my facts." Winston Churchill (1874–1965)

The BSB binary companion of the Sun, along with a smaller planetary body (SSB$_1$) orbiting around the big one; may have been detected by infrared telescopes already. Another possibility might be that the intermittent infrared emissions are coming from a series of large "leaders" that precede BSB and SSB$_1$. Some of the recent comets and near-miss asteroid encounters may be in the leader category. But, the late arriving leaders that are the forerunners of the Sun's BSB binary companion may be far more impressive than the entities that are detected and observed initially.

A dark brown dwarf binary companion star with an orbital semimajor axis of approximately 50 billion miles could be proposed as the BSB entity. As the Sun's binary companion approaches perihelion, its velocity could exceed 150,000 miles per hour (portions of comet Shoemaker-Levy hit Jupiter with velocities in excess of 130,000 miles per hour). At those velocities, BSB and SSB$_1$ could be less than 15 years away. It would be almost poetic if we started detecting the larger entities in late 2012. December 2012 is the end of the Mayan calendar, signifying the passage (or death) of the old age, and the beginning of a new era. A massive brown dwarf hurling at us at a velocity of 150,000 miles per hour would certainly be a catalyst for a new age, new attitudes and a new way of thinking.

The large differences in some of the planetary inclinations, removal of water from planetary surfaces (Mars), magnetic field intensity reductions or anomalies (Mercury, Venus, Mars), the missing planet between Mars and Jupiter and retrograde motions of Venus and certain moons could all have been influenced by the combination of BSB and SSB$_1$ as they periodically passed through the Solar System, with their leading and trailing components. Some of the planetary rings and the asteroid belt could be the remains of moons that suffered impact with leaders, lagging elements or moons of SSB$_1$.

"Most secrets of knowledge have been discovered by plain and neglected men than by men of popular fame. And this is so with good reason. For the men of popular fame are busy on popular matters." Roger Bacon (1220–1292)

Observing and experiencing these cyclical events will be frightening. As BSB and SSB$_1$ approach, many of us will be praying fervently. While praying, some will promise anything. We will pray for long periods of time to be saved. Some of us will probably try to make deals with God, and various saints—and maybe we will even change some of our behavior patterns. But it may be too little, too late.

How sympathetic would God be to a religious belief system that treats Him like a bipolar disordered, fool and an erratic serial killer in the so-called sacred books, such as the Old Testament and the Torah? How can those of the Jewish race even talk of "purification" in the alleged "God ordained Holocaust" in the Land of Canaan, after witnessing and suffering the "Holocaust Purification" at the hands of the Nazis? Does anyone realize what the penalties are for those who make God an accomplice in murder and depravity?

How sympathetic will Jesus be to Roman Catholics who victimized Orthodox Christians with theft and murder, while wearing crucifixes around their necks. How sympathetic will Mother Mary be to those who raped and murdered Muslim women while wearing rosaries in their pockets? How sympathetic will Jesus and Mary be to those who killed Jews and Muslims using Their Good Names, while chanting "God is with us—?" Do these people realize who and what Jesus rejected? Do they know the meaning of the term "Anti-Christ?"

What kind of chastisement and fire is being prepared for those who teach that Allah only speaks Arabic, Allah allows honor killing, Allah condones the killing of unbelievers and Allah looks the other way when women are subjugated and suppressed. Have they made Allah; the Merciful and Beneficent One; into Allah, the merciless, intolerant, blood thirsty tyrant? Is Allah the same fool as Yaweh? Don't they realize that Jihad comes back a hundred-fold, a thousand-fold as a curse on their children and their culture? Don't they understand that they cannot ever become what they were, if they remain what they are?

"Ask forgiveness of Allah; surely Allah is forgiving, merciful." Koran (Sura IV: 106)

How much sympathy will the Great Spirit have for Native Americans who will not walk in the same path of one from another tribe, who celebrate the defeat and death of other tribes as they swept across the plains; who then complain about the brutality and corruption of the white savages who invaded and took their land. The white savages are just another barbaric tribe; bigger and more brutal. This cycle of invasion, conquest, dominion, subjugation and brutality has never been unique to any culture or race. It appears in large segments of Native American, African, European, Jewish and Asian history.

How sympathetic will God be to the Jew, Roman Catholic, Muslim, Native American, Hindu or Mormon who consider themselves to be "chosen." The last words these people may hear might be, "Do you really believe I am so cruel and deceitful that I would create diversity; that I would create so many differences; and then condemn and abandon all of them—but one? Am I the divine fool of your so-called sacred writings? You have all toyed with Me and insulted Me enough!"

Our collective behavior could attract the most terrible and "Final Solution." And the rest of the universe will not even notice that we are gone. If we prove to be unworthy, there could be one less malignancy, one less nightmare, one less imperfection and one less set of problems in the universe. The rest of creation will be just fine without us. If this is the destiny we reap, all of us on this earth will finally be "the Chosen Ones." We will all be the "One's Chosen" by our own collective deeds, destroyed by our own hands and obliterated by our own cold and hard hearts. Again, this is not the Wrath of God; this is the more devastating kind of wrath that we bring on ourselves.

This scenario could be wrong. But, to all of the "Chosen Ones" out there, do you all really want to "risk it?" Based on my estimates, we may have less than 20 years left, to think it over. It will be interesting to see the results of our collective decision, and to see what kind of destiny we inherit from the consequences of our attitudes and actions.

"Death will come, always out of season." Chief Big Elk, Omaha (1772–1846)

Whether we collectively make the right decision, or the wrong one; God, Jesus, Allah, the Great Spirit will be with us. They will give us support and love, even if we disappoint them. They will not abandon or forsake our immortal souls, as we have abandoned and forsaken Them. They are present at our beginning, and our end. But God, Jesus, Alaha, Allah, the Great Mysterious or the Great Spirit cannot encourage our depravity or our intolerance. Claiming to be "chosen," initiating Crusades and Inquisitions, ritual sacrifice, clergy and hierarchy abuses, Manifest Destiny, stoning a woman who has been raped, honor killing, decadence, intolerance and fraudulent entries into Scripture are all repulsive and blasphemous to a loving, merciful, benevolent and just God. God has forgiven much, and has given us many chances. But, if we become too malignant, God may not intervene to stop the horrible chastisement that we are attracting, or the awesome "final blow" that could be the response to our attitudes and actions.

So how mighty is God Almighty? It appears that God is so mighty, that He can show His concern for at least 100 billion galaxies, targeting one of 100 billion solar systems in each galaxy. And out of possibly 600,000,000,000,000,000,000,000 (or more) potentially intelligent beings in the universe, and out of 6,000,000,000 human beings on the face of this earth, God can address each one of us individually and say, "I love you! You and your neighbors are special to Me. I am with you. I am in you. And there is room for all of you with Me. I want to protect and guide you. Please give Me your attention. I need your cooperation and assistance. Trust Me! I have your best interests at heart! Please, trust Me—." There you have It. That is God Almighty, the One we have degraded, slandered, blasphemed, humiliated, used and accused as an accomplice in our crimes of religion. Is this the best attitude, treatment and relationship we can offer to God Almighty?

> *"In Pakistan, an average of two women die each day from honor killings, often with Allah's name on the lips of the murderer." "In Islamic countries, victims of rape are stoned to death for adultery." "Our problems did not start with the dastardly Crusades. The problems started with Muslims." "Islam, when did we stop Thinking? Why are your lives so small and your lies so big?"* Irshad Manji, from her book, *The Trouble with Islam*, (2003)

12. AS I GET CLOSER TO JESUS, WHY DO I DRIFT FURTHER AWAY FROM THE ROMAN CATHOLIC CHURCH?

When I was younger, my spiritual life was based on the love, respect and fear of a corporate structured God, Son, Holy Spirit; with a devotion to the Son's mother and step father. Throw in a few saints and a couple of deceased family members, and that was the Group who I thought of when I said my prayers. But something happened to me that changed this viewpoint. During an early spring snow storm in South Dakota, my car went off the road and careened down a very steep embankment (some would say, a cliff). Neither the car nor I were hurt.

As the car and I were sliding down that steep embankment, I felt that there was something in the car with me, something comforting, safe and caring. It did not matter whether I would be alive or dead within the next few seconds, because I knew I was going to be well taken care of. I was going to be all right. What was it that was giving me comfort in a moment when I should have been fearful of pain and loss? Was it the Great Spirit, or the Great Mysterious? Was it God, Alaha, Allah, Jesus or the Holy Spirit? Was it my little brother, who died many years ago? Was it that little boy who's presence I still feel to this very day, and take great comfort in knowing that he is still there? Or was it All of the above?

What I did not quite realize then, but know now, is that it was "All of the above." They are All not just "out there," and accessible only through some organized hierarchical structure headquartered in Rome, Mecca, Jerusalem or in the middle of some prairie. God, Allah, Jesus, Alaha, the Great Spirit, the Great Mysterious are All in and with me. They are in and with all of us. And there is nothing that any power in this world can do to take Them out. Nothing!

"Blessed is the person who has struggled, he has found life." Gospel of Thomas 58

In Matthew 28: 20, Jesus says, "I am with you always, even unto the end of the world." In Luke 17: 21, He says "Behold, the kingdom of God is within you." And in Thomas 3, Jesus says, "The kingdom of God is inside of you, and it is outside of you." These sayings are consistent with the true message of Christ. This message from Jesus has not been lost in the various attempts to dilute or pervert His teachings in order to satisfy the power structure of a number of jealous and intolerant corporate religious entities. If Matthew 18: 20 is translated from Aramaic, it appears to read as follows: "Wherever two or three gather in my name and light, in my experience of the shining universe; then the I Am is already there around, among and inside them (53)."

We are no less privileged or gifted than St. Paul who, in Galatians 1: 16 and 24, claims that God and Jesus are in him. What is true for St. Paul is true for all of us. God and Jesus are with you. God and Jesus are in you. We can certainly reject Them. But if we are receptive to Isaiah's Leper, He will never forget or reject us. Words cannot express the joy and comfort I felt when I finally realized where Jesus is, what He is and why He is there. What Jesus has taught us is that, without us, corporate religious entities have no power, no authority, no credibility and no meaning. Yes, I know where Jesus is. But what is He? Can we form a picture of Jesus, the Semite man, the teacher, the prophet, the rabbi? If Jesus is what we are selling (or buying), do we have any idea of what the "Product" is that we are trying to promote?

While teaching a graduate engineering design class, one of my students proposed a design project based on planning, structuring and financing a Christian rock concert. I told the student that his proposal was a little unusual for engineering design, but I was very interested in what he was trying to do. So I told him to go ahead with the project. He was very enthusiastic about the effort, and so was I. A week later I reviewed all of the project proposals in class with the students, and gave them some insight into the kind of thinking, imagination and rigor that should be part of a graduate level engineering design project.

"Don't be so humble. You are not that great." Golda Meir (1898–1978) to a diplomat

Many students tend to propose very limited one-dimensional ideas, with minimal analytical effort and no clear view of purpose or objectives. One of the student proposals stated simply "I want to design engines." So I said, "O.K., let's take this a little farther. Consider a design and analysis effort for a 600 horsepower engine, that will allow speeds in excess of 240 miles per hour for a sports car—and design the car so that it will not become airborne at those high speeds."

When it came time to discuss the Christian rock concert proposal, I asked the young man, "In music, you are often selling something; an idea, an ideal, an emotion, a thing, a place—What are you selling, and what kind of product are you selling?" His answer was, "I am selling the message of Jesus the Christ, through music." I replied, "Great idea, we can have a much higher quality learning experience if we can inject singing and dancing into the effort. So, What you are selling is Jesus, the message and the Man." "Yes," he said, "I'm selling Jesus."

With my next statements, he became momentarily speechless, and the whole class awakened from their comatose condition. I said, "Well, in your selling efforts, you need to make some choices. Are you selling Jesus, the young, six foot tall, blue eyed, blond and relatively uneducated Swedish looking man; with incredibly smooth skin and a muscular body? Or are you going to sell what is probably the real Jesus; the five foot tall, "uncomely," educated, dark skinned Semite Man who may have been in his 40's, and may have had a crooked or hunched back condition? At this point, the Muslim and Hindu students were smiling and nodding their heads up and down in approval. I continued, "If you are selling the Man's message, you are selling the Man." "But Who and What was (or is) this "Man"—six foot tall Scandinavian or five foot tall, dark skinned Semite with Hamite origins?" I knew I was on dangerous ground, talking about these matters, in depth, in a secular university environment. But, I thought, "What the hell, at least I have their attention—seize the moment!"

"The swiftest thing to fly is the mind. Those who know have wings." Hopi Indian wisdom

I have often heard from those caught up in the fervor of the Christ, "It would be wonderful to see Jesus, to hear his message and talk to Him?" Well, I am not sure that would be such a wonderful thing for many Christians. Are we truly ready to "see Jesus?" Are we ready to shed our preconceived notions of Jesus—notions nurtured by a corporate Roman/European religious propaganda machine; with its Roman/European paintings and statues; and accept Jesus at face value. According to Mark 16, Luke 24, and the Acts of John; Jesus could change form, so that people did not recognize him. Perhaps Jesus could appear to us as a six foot tall Scandinavian, either in person or on a shroud in Turin, Italy, just to make many of us feel more comfortable in our biased conditions and views. But, this more comfortable form would most likely not be a true representation of the original Jesus.

How would we treat a short, dark skinned, educated Jesus with His relentless exhortations? How would we treat the "unsightly" or "uncomely" Jesus described in Isaiah 53, or in certain parts of the very uncomplimentary *Toledoth Yeshu*? How would we treat this Man, who gave us freedom, love and hope?

Would we welcome and receive this particular Jesus openly, with warmth and joy? Or would we follow more along the lines of Isaiah 53, and treat Him as if He were a leper? Would we regard Him as "One struck by God and afflicted?" Would we "esteem Him not," "despise" Him and consider Him "the most abject of men?" If just a part of the history we read is true, the Roman Catholic Church has done far worse things to Jesus than just despising Him and treating Him as if He were a leper—far worse.

> *"Religion is a very very complicated subject. I come from a family who honestly believe Jesus Christ is black. Now, I know if I sent, or if my son or daughter sent, a picture of a black Jesus Christ to some white kid, all hell would break loose."* Rep. Maxine Waters, (CA). Hearing (before a subcommittee) on the Judiciary House of Representatives Committee, H.J. Res. 184, Religious Freedom Protection, July 23, 1996, Serial Number 123, U.S. Government Printing Office, Washington D.C. (1997)

13. WHERE CAN A DISSENTING CATHOLIC GO FROM HERE?

The title of a commentary in the June 18, 2004 issue of the National Catholic Reporter (pg. 23), written by Colman McCarthy, states, "Catholics Should Obey or Go." However, a significant amount of the response to McCarthy's statements by dissident Roman Catholics can be summarized by the following, "Hell, no! We won't go!"

One of the more interesting books, authored by another person who was inspired to seek and find, was written by the Pulitzer Prize-winning journalist, Jimmy Breslin (54). I read Breslin's book, *The Church that Forgot Christ*, with interest, sadness and emotion. His struggles and anger appear to be similar to mine. This man, who was a devout Roman Catholic, had to sever his ties to a Church he once loved. Breslin recoiled at the darkness and betrayal that has characterized this church, and "the horrors it has visited upon children." As he engaged in the seeking and finding of his own personal quest, Jimmy Breslin could not reconcile his faith with the reality of the Roman Church.

Some time after realizing that the Church of Rome is too corrupt for his spirituality, Breslin walks past a Roman Catholic Church. He wonders, "Should I stay away, or should I go in?" He vacillates. Two thoughts are always in the back of his mind, "I could stay in the church and write with compassion, forgiveness and a reliance on redemption. Or, I could follow Christ's attack on the money changers in the temple." He realizes that "his past prolongs his indecision." The crimes and corruption are too massive. They must be attacked! Jimmy's book can be read in one sitting. I could not put it down. When I read the last two lines of his Epilogue, I almost fell to my knees. As I read that last page of his book, I realized that, in my own religious struggles and quest, I am right where he is; I am not a bad man, and I am not alone.

> *"You can't always get what you want. But if you try sometimes, you just might find—you get what you need. Oh yeah!"* Mick Jagger and Keith Richards, from the song, "You Cant Always Get What You Want," © 1969 ABKCO Music, Inc.

Following the example of the likes of Fr. James Kavanaugh, Jimmy Breslin and Fr. Hans Küng; in order to make appropriate and reasonable choices for religious pathways, spiritual guidance and our relationships with our "neighbors;" we need to sift through a massive amount of religious propaganda, weed it out, and discover "the truth that cannot be hidden." We need to separate the wheat from the chaff (Matthew 13: 30, Luke 3: 17 and John 15: 6). We need to "seek—and find." And, with some effort, finding part of the truth can be done. On a short-term basis, corporate religion has been successful in hiding, obliterating, burning or modifying a small portion of God's true Word, or killing a small portion of the "essence" of the Great Spirit. However, no matter how hard they try, "the chaff" of corporate religion can never completely obliterate the message and meaning of God, the Word, Allah or the Great Mysterious. There is not enough fire on the face of this earth that would allow them to complete such a hideous act.

Jesus of Nazareth refused to be perverted or overwhelmed by the hierarchy of Jerusalem or the Roman Empire. And the last vestige of that corrupt, decaying and brutal empire, disguised in the rich garments and tapestry of an organized religion, cannot completely pervert or distort the basic teachings given to us by the One treated like a leper in Isaiah 53. Neither the gates of hell, nor the power of a Roman Church, will ever be successful in compromising the message of the Christ. In spite of all the perversions of religious documentation, canon law foundations and scripture, His message is still in there. And this is one of the reasons why Jesus tells us to "Seek."

"Repent! What do you say to those families that were betrayed by people they believe in? And what do you say to the children who were violated in mind and body?"—Lauryn Hill, musician, speaking out on sexual abuse by clergy during the December 13, 2003 taping of the annual Vatican concert. Some Catholic hierarchy complained that Ms. Hill's comments were rude. Does that hierarchy realize Ms. Hill is a messenger? Do they have any capability to recognize "the message?" Do they have any capability to realize Who gave her the message?

Therefore, let's see if we can seek, find and open some doors. Let's see if we can pull the basic Jesus out of the clutter that has been used to cloud His image and pervert His teachings. The basic commandment Jesus gave is that we "love one another" and "love our neighbor as ourselves." In Matthew and Thomas, Jesus taught us that He is in us and outside of us. Where two or three of us are gathered for His sake, He is there with us. Jesus was not secretive, and He was very critical of pompous hierarchy. Jesus taught that all were welcome, and He often welcomed those who were despised or shunned by society.

However, the Roman Church has never been very tolerant of those who are different. Some of the first acts of the Roman Church were to murder and destroy Christian sects that did not believe all the dogma of the newly formed Roman Catholic Church. The murder, looting, rape, pillaging, destruction and corruption continued in much more subtle and much more brutal ways as the Roman Church evolved. These actions automatically eliminate any credibility or linkage that the Roman Catholic Church might claim to have with Jesus, or His teachings. Also, the attitude concerning secrecy and covert action within the Roman Church and Gnostic movement would separate both of these belief systems from the teachings and message of Jesus.

Jesus said, "In my Father's house are many mansions (John 14: 2). Jesus indicated that there are many pathways to God. The pathways taken by the Muslim, Roman Catholic, Protestant, Native American, Buddhist, Hindu, etc., or any person who "loves his or her neighbor" and "seeks;" are all blessed, honored and rewarded by a just and merciful God. Many corporate religious interests try to side-step or obscure that particular message. This is attempted in the Bible, the Torah and the Koran. But the true message is there, in the written rubble of those books. And God, Allah, Alaha, the Great Spirit will not allow selfish, cruel, fundamentalist ideas to obliterate that basic truth. All are welcome, all are blessed, all are chosen and all are loved.

"For centuries, theologians have been explaining the unknowable in terms of the-not-worth-knowing." H.L. Menken (1880–1956)

So does this mean that faithful Catholics must totally abandon their Catholic beliefs? No! Not at all. Any attempt by Roman Catholic Church hierarchy to corrupt or pervert the teachings of Jesus, does not place any guilt or shame on a devout Catholic. There is no original sin here, or anywhere else.

The Catholic faithful do not inherit the sins of their Church. This would be the same as blaming all German citizens for the Jewish Holocaust, just because the citizens are German. Catholic faithful do not automatically become marked by the sins of their corporate religion. However, like the Germans, the Catholic faithful do inherit the confusion and some aftermath associated with the dreadful acts of their leaders, clergy and hierarchy. We can cite two examples. The Crusades have never ceased. The Crusades continue to this day. The brutality of the war in Bosnia was a direct consequence of that particular ugly endeavor. Also, the consequences of protecting and hiding pedophile clergy and hierarchy will place huge organizational and financial burdens on Catholic faithful for decades to come. The faithful are not guilty of these crimes, but they may have to contend with many of the burdens and consequences of these crimes.

The crimes committed by the Roman Church against the basic teachings of Jesus, and the crimes it has committed against humanity are the reasons why, as previously indicated in Chapter 1, I will have to remove the word "Roman" from my Catholic religious belief system. The actions of the Roman Church have proven time and time again that it is one of the bad trees bearing terribly bad fruit.

But there are many pathways within the Catholic belief system. If the entire Vatican complex were to be rent asunder and crumble to dust before us, would that prevent us from going to church? Would we stop praying? Would we completely disregard all of the sacraments? Would we cease believing? Would Jesus the Christ also crumble to dust?

"You are the people who are shaping a better world. One of the secrets of inner peace is the practice of compassion." Dalai Lama

When we recite the Creed, do we think of it as a prayer? Is it a pledge of allegiance, or is it another form of "Sieg Heil?" How much of that Creed involves the teachings of Jesus, and how much of it involves negotiations and coercion? Let us "seek—and find."

When we receive communion, do we think about what we are doing? Did Jesus say "This is my body, This is my blood?" Or did he say, as would be said in Aramaic (3), "This—my body, This—my blood?" Was Jesus engaging in the Pagan inspired transubstantiation theme; or was He using the bread and wine as symbols of His death? If Jesus comes down to us "from above," through the power and pathway of the Roman Catholic Church, then one could make some arguments for transubstantiation. But, as stated in Luke 17: 21 and Thomas 3, Jesus says, "The kingdom of God is inside of you, and it is outside of you." And in Matthew 28: 20, Jesus says, "I am with you always, even unto the end of the world." These statements from Jesus strongly indicate that there is no need for transubstantiation; because God and Jesus are already with us and in us. Let us "seek—and find."

Where is the real power of the Catholic faith, or Christian faith? Jesus said "Where two or three are gathered for My sake, I will be in the midst of them" (Matthew 18: 20). Jesus did NOT say, "Where two or three are gathered for My sake; as long as they pledge their allegiance to a Roman Corporate Church structure and hierarchy, as long as they pledge their allegiance to even the most grotesque and brutal papal authorities, as long as they give money and their time to support building funds and litigation expenses, as long as they forgive and forget church supported war crimes, financial misdeeds and pedophilia crimes; I will be in the midst of them." Keeping in mind the questionable insertion in Matthew 16: 18-19; we might ask ourselves; Who is the real "Cornerstone," what is the real "Rock," and who are the "rocks" of the community that follow the teachings of Jesus of Nazareth? Let us "seek—and find."

"The whole of life from the moment you are born, to the moment you die, is a process of learning." Jiddu Krishnamurti (1895–1986)

Do we follow the Semite teacher, Jesus of Nazareth? Or do we follow the Roman/European model of Jesus? Do we listen to the Jesus who taught us to love, think, seek and find? Or do we follow the rigid, whitened and dogmatically sanitized Roman/Medieval Europe substitute? Do we believe that Jesus operates outside of us, through one corporate Roman Church pathway, through one powerful and infallible intermediary that murdered, raped and plundered record numbers of its own? Or do we believe in a Jesus who initiated a belief system, based on love, tolerance and community? Let us "seek—and find."

Can we attend a church service, a prayer meeting, a mass or any religious gathering and do this in remembrance of Him? Can we meet with others and pray together? "Thank You Jesus for becoming one of us. Thank You for being with us." Can we gather with others and acknowledge our similarities and differences in belief, and simply remember Him? Can we take communion without making something complex and brutal out of something so simple and beautiful? Can we thank God, Alaha, Allah, the Great Spirit or the Great Mysterious for giving us life? Let us "seek—and find."

In early 2004, I read a wonderful little book authored by a man who I knew many years ago. His name was Alfred (55). I only talked to him a few times, once while he was a disk jockey for a Rapid City, S.D. radio station, and once several years later when he was traveling and dabbling in various business interests and politics. Al McDonald had a wonderful sense of humor. When Rapid City converted from operator assisted calls to the dial system, Alfred told his radio audience to cover up their telephones with wet towels overnight. He said that before converting to the dial system, the telephone company was going to clean the telephone lines by blowing them out with compressed air. And of course, without the towels covering the telephones, many phone company customers would have telephone line gunk and goo all over their house the next day. Sure enough, some people had towels wrapped around their phones that night. Alfred was a hoot!

"What else is nature but God?" Seneca (4 B.C.–65 A.D.)

As a radio disk jockey, Alfred had a very colorful cast of "characters" that would supposedly visit him in the radio station studio each night. With a talent for imitation, after playing a couple of hit records, some of the "characters" would come in and complain about their work environment. Alfred took on the personality of Sgt. Flowers, from the local air base. Sgt. Flowers was always reminding his men, "Now I want you all to go out there and pick up those ugly cigarette butts." After a few days, Sgt. Flowers shortened his request to "All right you guys, pick up your ugly butts."

You have to realize that this was the 1950's. The words "virgin," "mistress" and "seduce" from the 1953 movie, "The Moon is Blue," shocked audiences and raised the wrath of many church leaders and self proclaimed moralists for years. Bishops were manufacturing mortal sins on the spot. Was Alfred referring to cigarette butts, or was he referring to other kinds of butts? He never answered that question directly. He kept the radio listeners and radio station management guessing. Alfred always seemed to enjoy being a little on "the edge."

Alfred met many famous people. He was a talented and intelligent man—interesting and sociable. Alfred had his struggles. He struggled with his stature, his sensitivity and his alcohol. He was a highly creative comedian and visionary; and was full of good healthy mischief. Alfred had an incredible amount of beauty and music in his heart and soul. One day, while reading his book, I realized the depth, breadth and power of Alfred's inner beauty.

"Spiritual Doctrines which exalt combat are doctrines which degrade the human race. Societies which exalt criminal actions (i.e. Jihad, Crusades, Inquisitions, Holy Wars, etc.*) will suffer a rapid deterioration in the mental and spiritual condition of of their inhabitants." William Bramley, from his book, *The Gods of Eden* (1993)

*Added for clarification.

In his little book, Alfred wrote letters to many famous and not so famous people. He wrote to Henry Fonda, Ronald Regan, Jesus Christ, Joseph and Mary, Mother Theresa, Luciano Pavarotti, Jimmy Swaggart, Henry Kissinger, Judas Iscariot, Walter Cronkite, Elizabeth Taylor, Francis of Assisi, some family members—to name a few. But the letter, that I will always treasure, is the letter Alfred wrote to a man named Jerry.

Dear Jerry:

I was at Neil's Tire the other day when I looked over and saw you. The door of the large garbage container was open and you were crawling into it. The folks at the Little Brown Jug Liquor Store told me that you take empty wine and beer bottles and funnel their last few drops into a plastic container.

You seem to smile always and you wave each time you see me. Jerry, I know that the voltage from an industrial accident has hurt your brain. I'm powerless to help you except to pray that instead of people making fun of you, they'll smile and wave back out of love.

Easy does it, Jerry.

Sincerely yours,

Alfred

I have had brief encounters with Jerry a number of times. When I saw Jerry, I did not have the same high quality reactions that Alfred had. I did not give Jerry the consideration that Alfred gave. I turned my head. I tried to make Jerry go away. I did not make fun of Jerry. But I was no better than those who did.

"Follow your bliss." Joseph Campbell (1904–1987)

Alfred and Jerry have each given me a gift, which allows me to see What and Who exists within both of them. In doing that, they enable me to see the spirit and potential that exists within myself. The difference between Alfred and me, is that when Alfred sees Jerry, Alfred feels compassion, love and concern. Alfred shines. Alfred is generous, inspirational and supportive. Alfred gives people like me something to strive for. Alfred reaffirms and provides an excellent example of one of the primary teachings of Jesus, "Love thy neighbor." Alfred and Jerry are my neighbors. And, Alfred is my standard. The heart, soul and spirit that Alfred possessed, is what I must strive to acquire.

Many insist that "we must all be like Jesus." Are they kidding? That is a frustratingly impossible objective. But this entire world would be a much more civilized, decent and happy place if we would all try to be like Alfred. It is the mindset and compassion of people like Alfred that will be the key to our collective survival. I believe with all my heart that Alfred's love and decency are powerful enough to change our destiny. Alfred's spirit can move a mountain—or deflect a dark star.

The difference between Jerry and me, in many ways, is precious little. We have a lot in common. But, Jerry is much friendlier and more content than I am. He is also a better teacher. It is apparent that we have portions of our brains that have been shocked, injured and rendered inactive. Unlike Jerry, my injuries and damaged response capabilities are superficial and reversible. Jerry provides wake-up calls for me. My treatment of Jerry, and my lack of consideration for him, are reminders of my insensitivity, lack of love and lack of compassion. I know that good qualities are there, inside me. As Jesus, Thomas and Luke have done, Jerry also communicated this message to me. He did this a long time ago, when he smiled and waved at me. Although I gave him nothing in return, Jerry gave me attention and friendship. In the best way he could, Jerry was demonstrating to me the behavior that reflects the teachings, concern, generosity and love that Jesus gave.

> *"Do not dismiss lightly the great gift of God's grace that lives in those in anonymity; neither make gods of those who sparkle for a time, whose sparkle may blind you to the goodness of God which is in them."* from the book *Alfred* (1983), by Al McDonald

The process of seeking and finding does not involve following straight and narrow pathways. The process often does not seem to make sense. The "pathway" is often the one that we have to make ourselves, and it can have many twists and agonizing turns. In some cases, it is difficult to see where to start or where to go. But, I will follow the recommendations of Jesus, and I will "Seek—." What I found in the third phase of my quest was Alfred and Jerry. I found their beauty, grace and strength. Alfred gave me solid directions. He supported the teachings of Jesus by giving me an excellent standard that I am able to follow. Alfred does not criticize my personal weaknesses or my dissent. He says, "Go ahead and turn right into the wind George. If you wish, be the heretic. Ride out that storm. But stay the course."

After listening to Alfred's recommendation, I would probably look at him and say, "If I stay the course, What happens if they hate me? What can I do if they reject me? What can I do if I go to church, and they tell me to leave? What can I do Alfred?" Alfred might reply, "George, what do you care? Don't be such a damn whiner! If they ask you to leave—then leave! And as you leave, shake off the dust of that place from your feet. And, be sure you leave before the collection plate is passed around. Easy does it, George. Quit worrying so much! You are going to be all right."

Yes! I think that is fairly close to what Alfred would say.

Jerry complements Alfred. Jerry confronted my fears, biases, preconceived notions and arrogance in a very soft way. Jerry demonstrated to me the power of God within him. He displayed God's gifts of love, grace and insight that are within him, and within all of us. When Jerry smiled at me and waved, I turned away. How I would love to live that moment over again. With God in him, and Jesus standing at his side, Jerry waved and smiled. I apologize to you, Jerry. Although I did not see the Three of You then, I can see All Three of You now.

"Intuition will tell the thinking mind where to look next." Dr. Jonas Salk (1914–1995)

14. THE NINTH LEPER

Then, as He entered a certain village, there met Him ten men who were lepers, who stood afar off. And they lifted up their voices and said, "Jesus, Master, have mercy on us!" So, when He saw them, He said to them, "Go, show yourselves to the priests." And so it was, as they went, they were cleansed. And one of them, when he saw that he was healed, returned, and with a loud voice, glorified God. And he fell down on his face, at His feet, giving Him thanks. And he was a Samaritan. So Jesus answered and said, "Were there not ten cleansed? But, where are the other nine? Were there not any found who returned to give glory to God except this foreigner?" And He said to him, "Arise, go your way. Your faith has made you well." Luke 17: 12-19

When I read this Gospel, I often think that there might be more to this story. I often think about a ninth leper, who was so excited about being cleansed, that he simply forgot everything and was literally dancing in the streets for days. After some period of time, the ninth leper finally realizes that during this wonderful exciting time, he was given a new life, but he forgot to thank the Man who made him well. So, the ninth leper goes on a quest to find Jesus and thank Him for the precious gift He gave. He searches continuously. He gets close. But, he always seems to be just a few days behind Jesus and His followers.

Then one morning, as the ninth leper approaches Jerusalem, he notices activity on the top of a rather grotesque looking hill. He watches, but his mind is elsewhere. The ninth leper is focused on his search to thank the Man who cleansed him and saved him from a living hell of disease and despair. He also wants to be in Jerusalem for the Sabbath.

"Heaven will be inherited by every man who has heaven in his soul." H. Ward Beecher (1813–1887)

As the ninth leper approaches one of the gates of Jerusalem, he notices more activity at the top of the hill. From a distance, he watches the chaos and effort as, several crosses are pulled up. He hears a loud "thud" as each cross slides into place.

The ninth leper listens carefully. As he approaches, even at that distance, he can hear the coarse talk and shouting of the Roman soldiers as they complete their gruesome task of crucifying trouble makers, political extremists and criminals. The ninth leper pauses for a moment, and thinks to himself, "May God have mercy on those three unfortunate souls. What could they have done to deserve this?

Under the watchful eyes of several Roman soldiers, who appear to be Syrian conscripts, the ninth leper passes through one of the outposts located some distance outside the Jerusalem gates. People are selling fruit and vegetables from their carts along the road as they approach Jerusalem. The ninth leper rests for awhile, and has his meal. He has a strong feeling that the Man who healed him might be in Jerusalem. He is full of hope and anticipation. "Maybe I will see Him today. Then, I will be able to properly thank Him for the gift of life He gave me. Perhaps this Man they call "Rabbi" will have something more to teach me. I want to hear His message and pass it on to others." As the ninth leper continues to walk, he notices that the sky is darkening. He walks past the pathway leading up to the top of the ugly grotesque hill. He shudders and does not want to even think about what is happening up there. But soon, he will know.

Thinking aloud, the ninth leper says softly, "I hope I eventually find this Man called Jesus. I want to show Him my appreciation and gratitude. Perhaps, I will see Him and talk to Him today." As the ninth leper walks past the pathway leading up to the top of the "Hill of the Skull," he has no idea that several events will occur in rapid succession. In a few minutes, he will finally see the Man they call "Rabbi." And the ninth leper will come down from that hill with a message.

"We ought to obey God rather than men." Acts 5: 29

When I was eight years old, I stole a Flash Gordon pistol from my friend, Buzzy (His name was LeRoy, but we all called him Buzzy). I loved that pistol, and I loved the way it sparked and buzzed when I pulled the trigger. It was a thing of beauty. And friendship-be-damned, that Flash Gordon pistol was something I had to have.

A few days later, Buzzy caught me with the stolen item in front of all our friends. I was frozen with fear and remorse. At that moment, Buzzy could have destroyed me. He could have embarrassed me and totally devastated my already questionable standing and reputation in our third grade community. He could have exposed me for being the little thief that I was. But Buzzy did not do this. Instead, Buzzy said, "Hey, O'Clock, how do you like the pistol I gave you? I knew you would like it." As everyone milled around and talked about things that were of concern to eight year olds, no one was aware of the mental turmoil, and subsequent relief, I had just experienced. Buzzy smiled at me and walked back into school. I was so relieved and grateful that I almost passed out. Buzzy had just given me forgiveness and redemption.

I was highly indebted to Buzzy. Many times, I contemplated the nobility and impact of his decency, kindness and tolerance. But years later, I could not believe what I overlooked. Buzzy gave me several precious gifts. But through all of my remorse and relief; I totally forgot to thank Buzzy, and return the stolen Flash Gordon pistol to him. In my relief, I was so far into myself, that I forgot about Buzzy!

When I was nine or ten, during a very troubled time in my life, an older boy named Howie called me over one day and said, "O'Clock, at times, you are a pain in the ass. But for the most part, you are all right. You are O.K." I was stunned. I was all right, and O.K.! Imagine that! Howie, had almost three additional years of age and wisdom on his side. So his compliment had to be valid. I cannot adequately describe the importance of the positive impact that Howie had on the rest of my life. He gave me acceptance and hope. But, again; in my relief and elation, I forgot to thank Howie for the valuable gifts he gave me.

"Shoot for the moon. Even if you miss it, you will land among the stars." Les Brown

Fifty six years later, I was lamenting to some close friends about my two failed marriages, and certain aspects of those two relationships. My friends both started to encourage me to learn from the experiences, and move on. Then, they both collectively said something that was an echo from the past. They said, "Yes, George, at times you do test our patience. But we love you. You are our dear to us. You are all right, you are O.K.!" As I listened to them, I could see the Power within them. I could see the direct link between Buzzy, Howie and those two close friends; a link that was impervious to the effects of time and space. These events were all connected, all loving and all sacred; giving me an important message during another critical time in my life.

There have been hundreds of acts of kindness and generosity that were given as gifts by people very close to me; family, friends, teachers, acquaintances and at other times, gifts from perfect strangers. They gave me life, hope, comfort, friendship, redemption and inspiration. But in my elation and relief, I failed to show a full appreciation for the sensitivity, generosity and love of those who gave the gifts. What came out of everyone of these people, young and old, was the grace and presence of God, Who is within them. When they gave the gifts to me, I was too concerned about myself to understand what was really happening. It took me a long time to understand that my gratitude and sensitivity need serious improvements.

Many years ago, I began to think about the real meaning of Luke 17: 12-19. In a healthy way, that part of Luke's Gospel haunted me. As I thought about the verse and read it over and over again, I asked myself, "Could there be more to this story?" My imagination took over. As the rest of the story developed in my mind, it didn't take long for me to realize the obvious—I am the ninth leper.

"O Great Spirit, whose voice I hear in the winds, I come to you as one of your many children. I need your strength and your wisdom. Make me strong, not to be superior to my brother, but to be able to fight my greatest enemy: myself." Chief Dan George, Salish (1899–1981)

I do not have the qualities and sensitive spirit of the tenth leper. I do not have the grace and heart of Alfred, Buzzy, Howie, Jerry, friends, parents, teachers and countless others who gave support, concern, love and encouragement when I needed it. But, I have at least one saving attribute. As an eight year old and as a sixty five year old, I know Who and What is working through all of these people. It is the Power and Grace that resides in them, and in me. The only way I can even come close to repaying them, and show my appreciation for the gifts they gave me, is to let you know what they have done. We wield tremendous power and influence over the lives of our neighbors. That is why loving those neighbors is so important.

I am the ninth leper.

I am the neighbor that has been loved, and the neighbor who should give love in return. I have work to do. I have been given many gifts including life, relationships, health, education, opportunity, insight and well being. But, what have I given in return? Who benefits from my existence? What treasure can I pass on that can even come close to the treasures given to me by Alfred, Buzzy, Howie, Jerry, my parents and many others? How do I honor them, and the God Who is within them? How do I honor them, and He, Who is with us, "even to the end of time?" How do I give honor and thanks to Isaiah's Leper, Jesus of Nazareth, Who has "borne our infirmities and carried our sorrows; One thought of as a leper, One struck by God and afflicted."

In some ways, am I one of those who has betrayed and ignored God, in me? Have I betrayed Isaiah's Leper? As I direct my criticism at the scandalous deeds of Roman Church hierarchy, am I the hypocrite? Am I another blind fool? Have I looked the other way, ignoring actions that violate decency, moral standards and teachings of the Christ? Have I participated with the cruel Inquisitor and Crusader to justify iniquities, arrogance and the struggle for power over others?

"Try not to become a man of success, but rather become a man of value."
Albert Einstein (1879–1955)

Defective as I am, I have been cleansed, enabled and forgiven—born not in original sin, but born in original goodness. I am a small part of a very large sacred body, one, of many, with a message. That simple collective message comes from the God within us, and the Savior Who is with us. We offer painful reminders for organized religion. We are reminders of what these religions have become—what they could have been—and what they will have to be, in order to have any credible link to God, Alaha, Jesus of Nazareth, Allah, Isa or the Great Spirit. There may be little time left for the Harlot of Babylon, the Woman Who Rides the Beast, the descendants of Constantine, the Tyrants of Mecca, the first Americans or the Conquerors of the Land of Canaan to mend their ways and avoid attracting a "Great Chastisement." In this book, I have described just one possible scenario for that awful encounter.

Like many dissenting Catholics, my religious position is not completely defined at this point. But I have a very good idea of just which parts of that religion must be avoided and rejected. In many cases, what must be rejected is easy to see. I simply ask myself, based on His teachings, what would Yeshua reject? What are the elements of Roman Catholicism that would horrify, anger and repulse Jesus of Nazareth?

Some answers to these questions have been provided by various comments from dissenting Catholic priests, nuns and laity. Their collective outrage appears to reflect the outrage and disappointment that the God within them feels; and it seems to reflect the feeling of betrayal that Jesus would feel. Many of these very spiritual people have pointed out that that "the Roman Church's ecclesiastical culture is amoral, criminal, delusional, perverse and riddled with rot and hypocrisy." There is a "pathology of silence, secrecy and deceit." The Roman Church has "abandoned God and victimized the innocent." The Roman Church, from its inception, has had a chronic problem with "sinning against the Holy Spirit."

"Him who comes to me, I will not cast out." John 6: 37

As a concerned Roman Catholic stated in the May 10, 2002 issue of the National Catholic Reporter, "I have little hope that any lasting reform can come from a group of men, the church hierarchy, who have absolutely no reason to become accountable or responsive. The structure of the Roman Catholic Church, supported by many people who seem to need an infallible hierarchy, will survive scandal and leave unscathed the guilty members of the hierarchy who perpetuate corruption. There is an inherent intractable weakness in the Roman Catholic Church that encourages the sin of pride among the clergy, and the attendant sins of arrogance, denial and corruption. How does a reflective intelligent person adhere to such a tradition?"

If even half of the comments from concerned Catholics are valid; those comments verify that the corrupt, despotic, self-centered and brutal influence of the Roman Empire must be ripped out of the Catholic religious structure. The Nicene loyalty oath must be abandoned. Rome must go—the sooner, the better. Roman influence has perverted basic Christianity long enough. As long as Rome maintains its grip on Catholicism; historical records and recent news indicate that Roman Catholicism could become even more decadent, criminal or corrupt. Apparently, it can't help itself—simply because it is Rome!

The Roman Catholic religion, in its corporate form and with its corporate policies, is totally incompatible with a genuine Christian spirituality—and it has been totally incompatible since its birth and establishment by Constantine in the fourth century. Many Roman Catholics, who are appalled at the scandals of their hierarchy, still feel comfortable in the Roman Church because of the advertised tradition that identifies the Roman Catholic Church with Jesus of Nazareth, St. Peter and St. Paul. If they do as Jesus requests, and "seek," many of these Roman Catholic faithful will be shocked with what they find. They will find out that the Roman Church's links to Jesus, St. Peter and St. Paul often appear to be based on fraudulent claims and document modifications—a cruel hoax if there ever was one.

"Sometimes a scream is better than a thesis." Ralph Waldo Emerson (1803–1892)

Roman Catholic faithful will find that they are following dogma and participating in liturgy and prayer that were often introduced through coercion, extortion and slaughter. This was, and still is, "the Roman way." The Catholic Church carries on with the belief system, corrupt behavior and traditions of its Roman origins, "obey or die."

How can the Roman influence be ripped out of Catholicism? Part of the answer to this is quite simple. Do not give Rome any money! In doing this, one has to be careful not to hurt those in need. However, the laity must control the finances—all of it. We can go to church, and acknowledge the respect that we have for our common faith and trust in the teachings of Jesus and his example. We can provide enough money to the local parish to keep the furnace and air conditioner working. We can give enough to support construction needs. We can support schools that provide education and job opportunities. We can support organizations that provide shelter for runaway kids. We can support the religious order that provides support, comfort and dignity for some of our Hindu neighbors, who often face a lonely and painful death in the streets of Calcutta. We can do this, and much more. But Rome should not receive one dime of our money. In order to survive, Catholicism cannot tolerate any Roman participation, manipulation, bullying, corruption, accounting games or extortion attempts.

If Catholicism is to survive, Catholics cannot recognize any Roman Church hierarchical claims, or take any Roman Church hierarchical authority seriously. Collectively, Roman Church hierarchy have failed to meet the requirements of I Timothy: 3, 1-13. Keep in mind, I Timothy is not an ideal or goal. It provides a clear set of reasonable specifications for a hierarchy position. I Timothy has not been consistently honored or recognized by the Roman Church since the Roman Church was initiated in the fourth century. This lack of attention to the hierarchical specifications of I Timothy invalidates all papal and Roman Church claims to authority, preeminence or grace.

"For it is within you that the Son of Man dwells. Go to Him, for those who seek him find him." The Gospel of Mary Magdalene 8: 19-22

In our attempts to prevent religious dogma and structure from perverting our spirituality, we need to recognize the monstrous actions of a Roman hierarchy that did not hesitate to slaughter millions of Christians who were judged to be faulty in their beliefs and customs. We should recognize the traps that are often set by hierarchy, and others, who engage in religious or spiritual abuse (56). Religious or spiritual abuse statements are easy to recognize and identify. Some of them are not very subtle: 1) Your questions reveal a lack of faith, 2) Do not question my (our) authority, 3) The only pathway to salvation is our pathway, 4) We alone are right! Others are quite subtle. Based on our standards and view: 1) You need to repent of your rebellion against God, 2) Strange are the ways of the Lord, 3) Your place in heaven will be determined by your good works and how pleasing you are in the eyes of God, 4) This dogma is a mystery, and can only be accepted by your strong faith in God (or Allah, or Jesus or the Great Spirit, etc.).

When power is postured and religions performance requirements are legislated, watch out (56)! Remember how the legislators in religious hierarchy are described in Matthew 23: 4: "And they bind together heavy and oppressive burdens on men's shoulders; but not with one finger of their own do they choose to move them." The blind fools, vipers, hypocrites that Jesus addressed in Matthew 23 seem to behave like a malignancy. For example, it is almost poetic that Boston's Cardinal Bernard Law was given a comfortable position in Rome after his participation in the pedophilia cover-up scandals was revealed. Law and other Roman Catholic prelates (including the papacy), who acted irresponsibly in the pedophilia cover-up, are exhibiting the same characteristics as cancer cells. They are aggregating and sticking together to form a tumor. And the necrotic, decaying and self-serving center of that tumor appears to be Rome.

"The Papacy is not other than the ghost of the deceased Roman Empire, sitting crowned upon the grave thereof." Thomas Hobbes (1588–1679), From his book, *Leviathan*

We should also recognize the difference between genuine prayer and a loyalty oath. In good conscience, I can only recite approximately 30% of the Nicene Creed. As Christians, we should educate ourselves concerning the number of people who were victimized and slaughtered over many of the basic components in that particular loyalty oath. Many priests and ministers have stated that there is nothing of Jesus in this Creed. The Nicene Creed was part of an effort to blend Pagan and Christian ideology into one basic state religion; and the methodology that was used to do this was often subterfuge, bribery, coercion and murder.

Do we really want to embrace the belief that God or Allah or the Great Spirit will only talk to a chosen few? With approximately 6 billion people on Earth and approximately 100 billion galaxies in our universe, are we going to give our particular deity the reputation of a Father who has children, and abandons almost all of them? When we meet our God, how are we going to explain that kind of slander and blasphemy? Roman Catholics are not the only ones who will have to address these questions. Of those who follow the Islamic faith, only 13% are Arabs (57). Allah may ask them, "What is the perverse logic behind the claim that Allah only hears prayers in Arabic." Everything that Allah created is "excellent." If that is true, then all languages and all people are "excellent." To state anything different is to blaspheme against Allah.

Do Catholics and Muslims really want to hang on to the belief that God, Allah, Jesus or Isa would abandon small children, or good persons, who follow other belief systems? Did God, Allah, Jesus or Isa make these kinds of statements, or could those kinds of statements have self-serving human origins? God created an incredibly diverse universe that encourages many belief systems. Did God make mistakes and introduce design flaws? Do we want to continue to insult our God and His Apostles by describing Them as incompetent, the ultimate discriminators, the cruel Deities and Apostles who simply toy with us?

"Ask her to wait a moment I am almost done." Carl Friedrich Gauss (1777–1855) While working, when informed that his wife is dying

Jesus and Paul both warned that one of the worst dangers to the faithful (or "the flock") was from "those among us." "Beware of men," "savage wolves," "speaking perverse things" in "the house." (Matthew 10:16, Acts 20: 29-30). From its beginnings, the wolves of Rome seem to have engaged in an endless variety of savagery and perversity.

Jesus has been used, and accused, in the manufacture of some ghastly statements. But, Jesus of Nazareth's real requests are simple. He wants us to "love" and to "seek." Anything that gets in the way of those two requests must be tossed out of our lives. Neither God, nor Jesus of Nazareth, guarantee that we will receive human love in return. They did not specify what we will find when we seek and they did not identify the specific conclusions that we will reach when we seek and find.

Jesus told his followers to "Seek—and Find." There can be no compromise on this request. Any hierarchical body that interferes with this sacred duty is automatically anti-Christ. Jesus did not write a book containing pat answers that he wants us to memorize. Jesus gave us some simple prayers, His saving grace, some flexibility and forgiveness (if we screw up) and great love. If more clarity is desired, I recommend obtaining advice on how to "seek" from a Native American who has experienced a "quest" or a sweat lodge. We must appreciate the amount of physical, mental and spiritual focus that they maintain with their efforts. Listen to some of the decisions these people have made during a deeply spiritual time of their lives. They don't sit in a pew memorizing Catechism questions and answers. They do not rely on a corporate religious conduit, representing some distant Great Spirit, to deliver forgiveness for their sins and iniquities. No! These people definitely seek and find. And their effort to seek and find is often not a comfortable experience. The agonizing questions they have to ask on their own, and the disturbing answers that are delivered, involve a direct interaction with the Great Spirit that is within them. There is no hierarchy, there are no middle-men, and there are no simple answers for them.

"If you want to make an apple pie from scratch, you must first create the universe." Carl Sagan (1934–1996)

I am the ninth leper. And I have a message.

I think of the messengers who have provided the Roman Catholic Church with ample warnings. Each messenger is unique. I admire their strength and their grace. I do not consider myself to be their equal. But the same God Who is within them is within me. My message to the Roman Church is an addition to theirs. It is based on what is in plain sight, and it is based on a few simple questions.

Roman Church hierarchy! Does Isaiah's Leper have to come into your rooms, offices and hallways with a whip? Does He have to physically drive you out, as He did with the money changers in the temple? Does He have to face you as He did with the scribes and Pharisees and identify you as blind fools and hypocrites? Do you think that a Man who said that the first will be last and the last first will have much tolerance for a corrupt and decadent hierarchy, much less any tolerance for a wide variety of crimes, depredations and negligent acts, all done in His sacred Name?

Roman Church hierarchy, do you need to have a massively destructive entity on a direct path toward your church steeples before you change your Godless ways? What does it take to make you realize the consequences of your denial and self-deception? You have the alleged murder of a recent pope—revelations of financial scandals—revelations of fraudulent excesses—revelations of massive sexual misconduct with children—revelations of avarice—revelations of depravity—revelations of a wide variety of criminal acts—revelations of war crimes—. These ugly dark deeds are not enough? Do you need a more direct message? Well, hang on to your cassocks reverend fathers, because there just might be another powerful entity, heading in your direction, that will be more than a match for the horror and darkness you have supported, nourished and promoted.

"*Hell is paved with the skulls of priests.*" French wisdom

In addressing Roman Church hierarchy, I would suggest that their highnesses might take some time to read Isaiah 54 and 60. Then, they should recognize that they have not been "the instrument for His (Jesus) work." They are not the power that can resist any "weapon that is formed against thee." Roman Church hierarchy appear to be a closer match to the "tongue that resists" and the entity that will be "condemned." If the Roman Church wants to identify "the beast" of Revelations, they do not have far to look. They should recognize that what they have done was prophesized in Jeremias 23 and 24. The collective actions of the Roman hierarchy brings them much closer to the "false prophets," those "perverse in their own hearts," and "strengthening the hands of the wicked." The Roman Church hierarchy seems more in alignment with the bad figs of Jeremias 24.

The June 20, 2003 issue of the National Catholic Reporter states that nearly 40% of Catholics polled by The Boston Globe said that they "would support, as a future step, splitting the American Church from Rome." Apparently, the primary motivating factor for schism is frustration (58). Many analysts believe that there is no U.S. bishop that has the strength or the level of moral conviction necessary to initiate a schism that will promote a separation of the American Catholic Church from Rome. Their analysis may be based on correct assumptions, but their conclusions would appear to be incorrect. Eventually, Catholic America will have to break away from the grasp of Rome, simply in order to survive. Rome has proven itself incapable of representing or following anything close to the teachings and example of Jesus of Nazareth. In order to save its own soul, the American Catholic Church will have to break away from the last remnant of a corrupt and brutal Roman Empire, a remnant that is an antithesis of the Christ.

Roman Church! I am the ninth leper. I am one of many. I have a message for you. And, you will not like it.

"*It is finished.*" John 19: 30

REFERENCES

1. Greeley, A. (Fr.), *The Catholic Myth: The Behavior and Beliefs of American Catholics*, Simon and Schuster, New York, NY (1997).
2. Kavanaugh, J. (Fr.), *A Modern Priest Looks At His Outdated Church*, Simon and Schuster, New York, NY (1968).
3. Küng, H. (Fr.), *The Catholic Church: A Short History*, Random House, New York, NY (2001).
4. Muller, H., *The Uses of the Past*, Oxford University Press, London (1952).
5. Ellerbe, H., *The Dark Side of Christian History*, Morningstar and Lark, Orlando, FL (1995).
6. Carroll, B.W. and Ostlie, D.A., *An Introduction to Modern Astrophysics*, Addison-Wesley Publishing Co., Reading, MA (1996).
7. Cohen, R., *Hearts Grown Brutal*, Random House, New York, NY (1998).
8. Smith, B., *What Went Wrong?*, Oxford University Press, Inc., New York, NY (2002).
9. Patai, R., *The Arab Mind*, Hatherleigh Press, Long Island, NY (2002).
10. Durant, W., *The Story of Civilization: The Age of Faith*, Simon & Schuster, New York, NY (1995).
11. Davidson, L., *Islamic Fundamentalism*, Greenwood Press, Westport, CT (1998).
12. Armstrong, K., *Islam, A Short History*, Random House, New York, NY (2000)
13. Picknett, L. and Price, C., *The Templar Revelation*, Simon & Schuster, New York, NY (1997).

> "I'm completely in favor of the separation of Church and State. My idea is that these two institutions screw up enough on their own, so both of them together is certain death." George Carlin

14. de Vries, H., *Religion and Violence*, Johns Hopkins University Press, Baltimore, MD (2002).

15. Richardson, D., *Secrets of the Koran*, Regal Books, Ventura, CA (2003)

16. Odea, T.F., *American Catholic Dilemma*, New American Library, New York, NY (1962).

17. Dolan, J.P., *Catholicism: A Historical Survey*, Barron's Educational Series, Woodbury, NY (1968).

18. Spong, J.S., *Why Christianity Must Change or Die*, Harper, San Francisco, CA (20030

19. Bronowski, J., *The Ascent of Man*, Little Brown and Co., Boston, MA (1973)

20. Gilbert, M., *The Holocaust: The History of the Jews of Europe During the Second World War*, Henry Holt, New York, NY (1987).

21. Vernadskey, G., *A History of Russia*, Yale University Press, New Haven, CT (1954).

22. Lord, L., "A Reign of Rural Terror, a World Away," US News and World Report, Vol. 134, p 4, July 7, 2003.

23. Küng, H. (Fr.), *Christianity: Essence, History and Future*, Continuum, New York, NY (1995).

24. John Jay College of Criminal Justice Report on "Sexual Abuse by Catholic Clergy,"February-March, 2004 (With excerpts from the National Catholic Reporter, February 27, 2004 and March 12, 2004).

25. Allen, J.L., "Polish Prelate Accused of Sexual Abuse, National Catholic Reporter, Vol. 38, p. 6, March 15, 2002.

26. National News, "Retired Vatican Official Pleads Guilty to Scam," National Catholic Reporter, Vol. 38, p. 16, September 20, 2002.

"We are all poor because we are all honest." Red Dog (19th century Oglala)

27. Williams, P.L., *The Vatican Exposed: Money, Murder and the Mafia*, Prometheus Books, Amherst, NY (2003).

28. Ryan, D., "One Bishop's High Cost of Living," National Catholic Reporter, Vol. 38, p. 6, October 25, 2002.

29. Allen, J.L., "Law in Rome; Gays in Seminaries; Cardinals in Waiting; a Canadian Bishop in Love," National Catholic Reporter, Vol. 38, p. 9, December 12, 2002.

30. Oddie, W., "Shock Waves That Still Rattle the Vatican," The Daily Telegraph (London), p. 8, August 8, 1987.

31. Yallop, D.A., *In God's Name: An Investigation into the Murder of Pope John Paul I*, Bantam Books, New York, NY (1984).

32. Tanner, M., *Croatia: A Nation Forged in War*, Yale University Press, New Haven, CT (1997).

33. McBrien, R.P., "Forgiveness From Sin, But Not Pardon for Crime," National Catholic Reporter, Vol. 39, p. 18, May 16, 2003.

34. Harrington, B., "Confronting Embarrassment and Shame," The Courier (Diocese of Winona, MN), Vol. 94, p. 2, June, 2003.

35. Allen, J.L., "1962 Document Orders Secrecy in Sex Cases," National Catholic Reporter, Vol. 39, p. 12, August 15, 2003.

36. Carroll, J., *Sword of Constantine*, Houghton Mifflin Co., New York, NY (2001).

37. Nelson-Pallmeyer, J., *Jesus Against Christianity: Reclaiming the Missing Jesus*, Trinity Press Intl., Harrisburg, PA (2001).

38. Wills, G., *Papal Sin: Structures of Deceit*, Doubleday, New York, NY (2000).

39. Chamberlin, E.R., *The Bad Popes*, Barnes and Noble Books, New York, NY (1993).

> *"We find (Catholic hierarchy), with some exceptions, unable or unprepared to deal with the issue of how to speak of God and Jesus in the light of contemporary scriptural studies or knowledge about the development of life on earth or any appreciation of the magnitude of our universe. They simply will not discuss it."* Michael Morwood

40. Pennington, K., "History of Canon Law: History of Jurisprudence, The Catholic Tradition," The Catholic University of America, Washington, D.C., Law 507, Canon Law 701, June, 2003.

41. Chodorow, S., "Dishonest Litigation in the Church Courts, 1140–1198, From: *Law, Church and Society: Essays in Honor of Stephan Kuttner*, Editors: Pennington, K. and Somerville, R., University of Pennsylvania Press, Philadelphia, PA (1977).

42. Jones, A., "Lawyer Struggles With His Church's Seamy Side," National Catholic Reporter, Vol. 38, pp. 11-12, December 20, 2002.

43. Gamow, G., *One, Two, Three—Infinity*, New American Library, New York, NY (1960).

44. Hoyle, F., *Frontiers of Astronomy*, New American Library, New York, NY (1960).

45. Simcoe, R.A., "The Cosmic Web," American Scientist, Vol. 92, pp. 28-37, January-February, 2004.

46. McDonough, T.R. and Brin, D., "The Bubbling Universe," Omni, Vol. 15, pp. 85-98, October, 1992.

47. Arkani-Hamed, N., Dimopoulos, S. and Dvali, G.,"The Universe's Unseen Dimensions," Scientific American, pp. 62-69, August, 2000.

48. White, J., *Pole Shift*, Doubleday, New York, NY (1980).

49. Freedman, D.H., "The Mediocre Universe," Discover, Vol. 17, pp. 65-75, February, 1996.

50. Kunzig, R., "Taking a Shot At Einstein," US News and World Report, Vol. 134, pp. 48-50, May 26, 2003.

51. Irion, R., "Sensing the Hidden Heat of the Universe," Science, Vol. 298, pp. 1870-1872, 6 December, 2002.

> *"Millions of Muslims around the world long for freedom, and they cannot be free unless more and more voices speak out the truth and expose the nature of a religion that has for centuries held its adherents in fear and bondage."*
> Reza Safa (Ref. 15)

52. Velikovsky, I., *Worlds In Collision*, Simon and Schuster, New York, NY (1977).

53. Klotz, N.D., *The Hidden Gospel*, Quest Books, Wheaton, IL (2001).

54. Breslin, J., *The Church That Forgot Christ*, Free Press, Simon & Schuster, New York, NY (2004).

55. McDonald, A., *Alfred*, McDonald Press, Rapid City, SD (1983).

56. Johnson, D. and Vanvonderen, J., *The Subtle Power of Spiritual Abuse*, Bethany House, Minneapolis, MN (1991).

57. Manji, I., *The Trouble With Islam*, St. Martins Press, New York, NY (2003).

58. Feueherd, J., "Signs of Distress," National Catholic Reporter, Vol. 39, p. 4, June 20, 2003.

QUOTATIONS

Some of the quotations in this book were obtained from Bartlett's Quotations. There are many excellent quotation sources on the INTERNET, including the web site of Dr. Gabriel Robins and various web sites that provide quotations from scientists and philosophers. The Akta Lakota Museum and Cultural Center of St. Joseph's Indian School, Chamberlain, S.D.; and the book *Native American Wisdom*, by Kent Nerburn and Louise Mengelkoch were excellent sources for a number of very profound and inspirational Native American quotations.

"We are a sinful church. We are naked. Our anger, our pain, our anguish, our shame and our vulnerability are clear to the whole world." Archbishop Alphonsus Penny, Newfoundland, Canada, resigning in response to a very scathing report on his mishandling of clergy sexual abuse in 1990

ABOUT THE AUTHOR

George Daniel O'Clock, Jr. has a B.S., M.S. and Ph.D. in electrical engineering, an MBA in finance and a Master's degree in biological sciences. He is a registered professional engineer in the states of California and Minnesota, a licensed commercial pilot (ASEL) and mildly competent with a bow and arrow. He is the co-inventor of six patents and has shown a modest amount of aptitude as a teacher in the areas of electrical engineering, physics, business and biological sciences. Some of his passions include electrotherapy research for cancer treatment, wound healing and other applications in cell biology and immunology. Dr. O'Clock has published and presented more than 80 papers in the fields of business, economic forecasting, biomedical engineering, solid state physics, semiconductor manufacturing, surface science, metallurgy, spectroscopy, communication systems, microwave systems and engineering education.

For some time, Dr. O'Clock has been integrating the fields of astronomy, biology and theology in some of the courses he has taught in several colleges and universities. This is not easy to do in secular institutions. Some of the material in this book is the result of research associated with part of that teaching effort.

978-0-595-35141-1
0-595-35141-7